The Silver Spoon
PUGLIA

THE GARDEN OF ITALY

The sister regions Puglia and Basilicata are probably Italy's best-kept secrets. Tucked respectively into the heel and instep of the boot of the country, they converge into an extraordinarily beautiful and varied landscape, ranging from the sun-kissed wheat fields of the Tavoliere in Puglia to the soaring peaks of the Apennine Mountains that extend as far north as Liguria, and to the densely forested interior of Basilicata that dips down to the enchanting Pollino National Park. From this last spot, watching the sun rise over the Ionian Sea and set over the Tyrrhenian Sea is one of life's greatest pleasures.

The culinary heritage of Puglia and Basilicata dates back more than 3,000 years, and remains among the most authentic in the entire Mediterranean basin. The two regions at one time formed a sizeable chunk of Magna Graecia (Greater Greece), thanks to ancient Greek colonists who arrived in the eighth century BC and made a lasting impact on the cuisine – and much else. Even today, in some of the smaller towns and villages, you can still hear the old Griko dialect being spoken. Subsequent invaders came from all over Europe, Africa and the Middle East, and all left their mark on the regional cuisine. Arabs, for example, introduced the exotic red aubergine (eggplant, see page 249), while sailors from the East Indies brought exotic spices, such as cinnamon and nutmeg. Now, in the twenty-first century, southern Italy is fast becoming recognized as one of the best places to eat, not just for the superb quality of its ingredients, but for honest dishes born of its cooks' endlessly ingenious capacity for making something out of nothing.

An early admirer of the region was Holy Roman Emperor Federico II of Swabia. A brilliant and remarkably open-minded man, he was credited with having embraced the cultures of many civilizations – Norman, Arab and Greco and Latin – and although his

Page 4:
The ancient town of Matera, Basilicata, is nestled in the lush valley of this ravine, known as *La Gravina di Matera.*

Pages 5–6:
One of the sights of the Itria Valley is the *trulli* dotted across the land. The dry, stone huts with their conical roofs add a distinct look to the landscape.

Cherries grow in abundance in the early summer months. Turi's Ferrovia cherries are coveted for their sweet, juicy flesh.

The captivating landscape
of the Murgia plateau
surrounds Matera.

court was in Palermo on the island of Sicily, he loved
the whole of southern Italy unconditionally. Indeed,
he was nicknamed *Puer Apuliae* (Pugliese Boy)
because of his passion for the place, and hosted
legendary banquets using the produce of the regions.
His right-hand man in all of this was a famous chef
of that time, Mastro Berardo, who prepared seasonal
dishes incorporating a riot of colours, spices and
aromas. Numerous courses of salads and fruits would
be followed by soups of spelt, and vegetables plucked
from the gardens of the imperial palace in Lucera:
these included borage, rocket (arugula), wild chicory
(see page 63) and *cardoncelli* (the wild 'king trumpet'
mushroom), boiled and dressed with olive oil. Federico
was particularly fond of *ingrattonato*, a rustic soup from
Basilicata, made from tripe and eggs.

After food, the emperor's second passion was hunting
with falcons for small game, especially woodcock,
which his chef would dress with sophisticated sauces
of honey and aromatic herbs. He also went after wild
boar, the breed from which the present-day famous
Lucania pigs are descended, and these would often
be roasted whole. Another favourite dish included
aschipescia (fried eels), freshly sourced from the salt lake
Lesina and served with *salsa scapece* (vinegar sauce).
Both are still typical antipasti in southern Italy. Altamura
bread (see page 137) is often served alongside them, and
Federico loved to eat this with provolone and pecorino
cheeses. His enthusiasm for the region and its cuisine
knew no bounds, and he once said: 'It is obvious that
the God of the Jews never knew this land, this natural
environment, otherwise he would never have given his
people Palestine as the Promised Land.'

Ironically, this great bounty is known as *cucina povera*
(literally 'poor kitchen'), an allusion to the locals' frugal
approach to food that could be summed up as making
the best of what was to hand. Far better, and more
accurate, would be to regard it as a celebration of the
prime ingredients that come from the land, forests and

Pages 12–3:
Bari, the capital of Puglia,
is home to one of Italy's
key ports. The abundance
of fresh seafood available
has heavily influenced the
region's cuisine.

waters. Take, for example, the pigs that roam the woodlands of Lucania in Basilicata: they yield not only celebrated salumi and sausages (see page 234), but also pork fat, an essential ingredient of *sugna piccante,* a sort of dripping, stored in glass jars and a useful quick lunch spread on bread. The result of the regions' straightforward and practical attitude to food is honest dishes that elevate simple ingredients to gastronomic excellence. Why else would plum tomatoes (see page 134), olives (see page 166) and mozzarella have spread around the world? Their use might have been rooted in native pragmatism, but their ubiquity now is thanks to quality and imagination.

Almost without exception, regional dishes include at least one of the 'holy trinity' of ingredients: wheat, olive oil and wine. The first of these is, of course, the basis of pasta, which figures large in local cuisine and home cooks still insist on making their own. Combined, the regions have at least 200 different types, each town and province having its own variation on a theme. Thus the *orecchiette* (ear-shaped pasta, see page 98) of Bari may be bigger, smaller or have more grooves than those made elsewhere, but the fundamental shape is the same. The constant is that pasta is the foundation of many iconic dishes, such as *Ciceri e trie* (Chickpeas [garbanzo beans] and tria, see page 199) and *Orecchiette con cime di rapa* (Orecchiette with broccoli rabe, see page 104). These humble dishes were once relied on to keep people going in lean times, but pasta can also be 'dressed up' for celebrations – hence dishes such as *Timballo di pasta* (Pasta timbale, see page 40), a layered dish of penne, meatballs and vegetables.

Italian cuisine would be unthinkable without olive oil, and some of the finest are produced in the south. Ranging from grassy and green to fruity and golden, they are used lavishly as an ingredient in their own right, not merely as a drizzle to garnish a dish, though that is important too.

The coastline of Puglia stretches for more than 800 km/500 miles and is known for its warm, clean waters that attract Italian and international holiday-goers alike.

The third member of the 'trinity' is wine, which is produced all over Puglia and Basilicata. The regions have a reputation for lusty, country wines, but as the local cuisines become better known, so too are the wines, and gradually gaining international critical acclaim.

With these three key ingredients alone, you can quickly have something approximating supper, but the regions' inhabitants have imaginations as rich as their surroundings when it comes to putting food on the table, so approximations really don't feature. As always happens between bordering regions, ingredients and ideas are widely exchanged. Staples common to both areas include exceptional dairy produce, plus broad (fava) beans, pork and lamb, but there are also key differences. Basilicata, unlike Puglia, makes almost daily use of hot chilli peppers, which has given rise to the local proverb: '*Lu paprini e lu pupon ie' lu pranz r' lu cafun',* meaning 'Sweet and hot peppers are food for country people'. This says a great deal about poverty in years gone by, although it should be remembered that chilli was also believed to treat and prevent malaria, which was a massive problem in the area for centuries.

The art of cooking is a proud tradition in Puglia and Basilicata. People seem to have an inherent ability to coax deeply authentic flavours from the local abundance of grains, vegetables, wild herbs and game. A full menu in either region would begin with several courses of antipasti, followed by pasta, a fish or meat dish, and a dessert. The whole repast is served with plenty of locally made wine (see page 48), and finished with a shot of local *amaro* (bitters) to aid digestion. Such meals are lengthy affairs of love and friendship. They are where life, at its most convivial, happens.

Pages 18–9:
The Murgese horse originated in the Murge during the Spanish rule. Bred and raised in a semi-wild herd state, they live outside year round and forage for food.

FOOD FESTIVALS

Desserts on display in one of many Martinucci stores across Puglia. A celebrated and traditional Italian pastry and gelato maker founded in 1950 by John Martinucci and his son, Rocco.

There is no better way to get to the heart of what regional cooking means to Italians than to attend a local *sagre*, or communal feast. These occasions are the backbone of just about any festival in Italy, and nowhere more so than in Puglia and Basilicata, where food is an integral part of identity. It is the glue that binds family and neighbours, friends and strangers, and any excuse to bond over a meal will do.

Each *sagre* trumpets a new crop of seasonal produce like it's the arrival of a much longed-for newborn. In early spring, for example, the first delicate *lampascioni* (grape hyacinth bulbs, see page 220) – addictive when frittered and fried (see page 222) – are dug up in vineyards. Sought out in markets with a gusto that only a Pugliese could understand, *lampascioni* are considered by locals to be superior to even the finest truffles. Hands are rubbed and lips smacked over authentic regional dishes, such as *Strascinati con pomodoro e basilico* (Strascinati with tomato and basil, see page 96). And for religious celebrations, such as Easter and Christmas, anything less than a *scorpacciata* – a huge, day-long banquet that marks the start of all important holidays – is simply bad manners.

These intensely social occasions look every inch the archetypal Mediterranean festival: trees are festooned in fairy lights, brightly coloured market stalls groan beneath the weight of edible goodies, and trestle tables and chairs are dragged into the streets and squares to form impromptu al fresco dining rooms. Festivals are times to eat, drink and be merry, and they happen almost weekly. On the following pages is a list of the principal ones in Puglia and Basilicata and what's eaten at them.

Pages 24–5:
Sunset in the town of Martina Franca, over looking the Itria Valley – home to Martina Franca's high-quality white wine.

FOOD FESTIVALS

JANUARY

Sagra del suino | Pig festival
Lucera, Foggia

FEBRUARY

Sagra del maiale nero | Feast of the black pig
Faeto, Bari

MARCH

Festa di San Giuseppe | St Joseph's Day
Throughout Puglia

APRIL

Sagra della cuddhura | Cuddhura (an Easter sweet)
festival
Santa Cesarea Terme, Lecce

Sagra delle arance | Orange festival
Vico del Gargano, Foggia

Sagra delle pappaiottule | Pappaiottule festival
Castri di Lecce, Lecce

Sagra dei tarallucci e vino | Feast of taralli and wine
Alberobello, Bari

MAY

Sagra della seppia | Squid festival
Margherita di Savoia, Barletta-Andria-Trani

Sagra te le puccia all'ampa | A festival of wood-
baked bread
Novoli, Lecce

Fera ti li cerasi | Cherry festival
Leverano, Lecce

JUNE

Negroamaro wine festival | Wine festival
Brindisi, Brindisi

Sagra del fioroni | Early fig festival
Fasano, Brindisi

Sagra della ciliegia ferrovia | Railway cherry festival
Turi, Bari

Festa del pane | Bread Feast
Altamura, Bari

JULY

Sagra te lu ranu | Summer food festival
Merine, Lecce

Sagra della frisa | Frisa festival
Matino, Lecce

Carnevale del brigantino | Brigatino carnival
Crispiano, Taranto

Strade golose | Local artisanal food and wine
Gallipoli, Lecce

Boccondivino | Local food and wine festival
Carovigno, Brindisi

Marangiane in festa | Aubergine (eggplant) festival
Castri di Lecce, Lecce

Sagra della frisa e del pesce fritto | Fresh and fried
fish festival
Gallipoli, Lecce

Festa del pasticciotto | Custard pie feast
Surat, Lecce

Sagra della polpetta | Meatball festival
Grottaglie, Taranto

AUGUST

Mercatino del gusto | Food market
Maglie, Lecce

Sagra della sceblasti | Festival of Greek-style foccacia
and tomatoes
Zollino, Lecce

Sagra del polpo | Octopus festival
Mola di Bari, Bari

Sagra del prosciutto | Prosciutto festival
Faeto, Foggia

Calici di stelle | Open-air wine tasting
Trani, Bari and Copertino, Lecce

Sagra delle orecchiette | Celebration of *orecchiette*
Cisternino, Brindisi

Sagra della percoca | Peach festival
Canosa di Puglia, Barletta-Andria-Trani

Sagra del caciocavallo | Festival of Caciocavallo cheese
Monteleone di Puglia, Foggia

Note di gusto | Food and wine-tasting festival
Palagiano, Taranto

Sagra della mozzarella | Mozzarella festival
Francavilla Fontana, Brindisi

Sagra del fagiolo | Bean festival
Sarconi, Potenza

Sagra del pesce spada | Swordfish festival
Savalletri, Brindisi

Mareviglioso | Fish and seafood extravaganza
Polignano a Mare, Bari

SEPTEMBER

Sagra del pecorino di filiano | Celebration of ewe's milk
hard cheese
Filiano, Potenza

Sagre della zampina e del buon vino | Feast of rustic
pork sausages and good wine
Sammichele di Bari, Bari

Sagra dei fichi secchi | Dried fig festival
Miglionico, Matera

OCTOBER

Sagra delle olive | Olive festival
Sannicandro di Bari, Bari

Profumi e sapori d'autunno | Fragrances and flavours
of autumn
Cassano delle Murge, Bari

Sagra de la volìa cazzata | Olive festival
Martano, Lecce

La Sagra del calzone | Calzone festival
Acquaviva delle Fonti, Bari

NOVEMBER

Festa del vino novello | New wine festival
Locorotondo, Bari

Bacco nelle gnostre | Wine and roast chestnuts festival
Noci, Bari

Sagra del fungo cardoncello | Cardoncello mushroom
festival
Ruvo di Puglia, Bari

Il cardoncello novello | New wine and *cardoncello*
mushroom festival
Gravina, Bari

Sagra del carciofo | Artichoke festival
Trinitapoli, Barletta-Andria-Trani

DECEMBER

Sagra della cartellata | *Cartellata* (a Christmas sweet)
festival
Trani, Barletta-Andria-Trani

Pettole nelle gnostre | Fried dough ball and
chocolate festival
Noci, Bari

Sagra della pittula | *Pittula* festival
Surat, Lecce

I

FOGGIA

FOGGIA

'*A chi è convinto che a tavolo non si invecchi*' goes a local
saying, meaning 'Eat well, and you'll never grow old'.
The region of Foggia is the northernmost province
of Puglia, encompassing the spur of Italy's boot and
the beautiful Tremiti Islands floating just off it like little
emeralds in a sapphire sea. In the thirteenth century
it was Emperor Federico II's favoured winter residence,
and the famous Rosati market has been going strong
ever since. Occupying an entire street of the oldest
neighbourhood in Foggia, it fills early each morning
with local farmers, fishermen, butchers and cheese-
mongers, as well as foragers of mushrooms and wild
herbs, shepherds and artisan bakers, offering up the
most dazzling cornucopia of produce in the land.

The market is partly surrounded by the Foresta
Umbra, the only remaining part of Italy's ancient
Black Forest, a favourite hunting ground of Federico's,
and so named because light could not penetrate its
dense growth. Nonetheless, it afforded many treats for
his table, including borage, wild mustard, wild fennel,
chicory (endive) and sow thistle. These were much
appreciated by Federico, whose cooks came up with
fogliammischiate – a wild herb salad with bacon. Another
of the emperor's favourite dishes was an antipasto based
on the eels hauled from the area's two saltwater lakes,
Lesina and Varano. The eels were chopped, dipped
in flour and fried, then stored in wooden barrels of
vinegar until they were needed.

Soon producers from all over Italy heard of the bounty
in Foggia, and started coming to market with their
Abruzzan hams and Sicilian wines. Even Federico
began raising his own chickens, ducks and geese, and
also planted new olive groves of the Ogliarola variety,
imported from Sicily. Today the Cerignola area is
renowned for its vast swathes of olive groves, rolling up
against the foothills of Monte d'Elio like silvery waves.

Page 26:
Cherry blossoms in
bloom. Puglia is well
known for its Ferrovia,
or 'railway', cherry.
Legend has it that the
cultivar was discovered
growing alongside a
railway track.

Tavoliere delle Puglie,
or 'Table of Puglia', is a
prehistoric seabed that is
now cultivated for wheat,
sugar beet, olives, grapes
and tomatoes.

They produce what many consider to be the best
table olives in the world – the legendary PDO
(Protected Designation of Origin) Bella della Daunia
olives – and renowned tomatoes. In fact, nearly every
canned plum tomato in Europe comes from Foggia,
about two million tonnes per year in total.

The Dauni Mountains' rich pasture and thick
woodland make this an excellent region for cheese
lovers too. Canestrato is made from a mixture of goat's
and sheep's milk and aged for a minimum of 60 days in
hand-woven wicker baskets and smoked *fagottini* comes
in cute little bundles. Excellent goat's cheese comes
from the pretty medieval village of Mattinata, where
shepherds make it in huts tucked into hidden folds
of the nearby hills according to ancient traditions.
It is sensational when drizzled with the sweet, fruity
Mattinata olive oil from the Ogliarola olive, creating
a snack that's about as 'locavore' as it's possible to get,
especially when paired with the wines of Lucera, such
as San Severo, Orta Nova, Daunia or Cacc'e Muitte.

Finally, there is the Tavoliere, the largest plain of
southern Italy, itself another sea of dancing yellow
cornfields that contribute so much to the cooking of
the region. *Tavolo* means 'table', a reference to both the
landscape and its role as the breadbasket of the country.
The most iconic local dish is *pancotto foggiano*, a classic
'something-from-nothing' soup based on stale bread,
old potatoes, wild rocket (arugula) or other greens, plus
extra-virgin olive oil thinned with a glass of country
wine. This represents local cuisine at its most pragmatic.

PANCOTTO

Bread soup

Preparation time: 30 minutes
Cooking time: 30–40 minutes
Serves 6

— 500 g / 1 lb 2 oz potatoes,
   cut into 5-mm / ¼-inch slices
— 1 onion, finely chopped
— ½ celery stalk, chopped
— 1 tablespoon chopped parsley
— 4 small tomatoes, chopped
— salt
— 1 kg / 2¼ lb turnips,
   cut into 5-mm (¼-inch) slices
— 500 g / 1 lb 2 oz stale Altamura
   loaf, sliced
— 2–3 tablespoons olive oil
— 1 small dried chilli, crushed
— 1 clove garlic

Put the potatoes, onion, celery, parsley and tomatoes into a saucepan, cover with cold water and bring to a boil. Add salt, then cover and simmer for 6–7 minutes, covered, until the potatoes are almost cooked. Add the turnips and cook until soft.

Soften the bread in the vegetable mixture for just a few seconds, then divide it among 6 bowls. Pour some stock and spoon some vegetables over each serving.

Heat the oil in a frying pan or skillet, add the chilli and fry briefly to release the flavour. Brown the garlic clove in the same pan, then remove it. Drizzle the flavoured oil over the soup and serve.

(The traditional recipe also includes 1 beaten egg per person. If you want to do this, add it to the softened bread in each bowl, then pour over a few ladlefuls of stock.)

AUBERGINES

In July local volunteers in Castri di Lecce organize the annual *Marangiane in festa*, a celebration of *melanzane,* or aubergines (eggplants), that lasts four days. During that time the search for the best aubergine-based dishes becomes a local obsession, and the question on everyone's lips, year after year, is: 'Can anyone really improve on the *melanzanata?*', a cousin of Sicily's more famous *caponata*. The answer is invariably a resounding 'yes' because aubergine is the most versatile of vegetables, especially in the hands of the Pugliese.

Aubergines were originally introduced to Europe by Arab invaders (probably via Spain) and quickly became a deeply integrated Puglian staple. Here it is used in many imaginative ways: simply rolled (aubergine [eggplant] rolls, see page 38); served as a side dish, preserved in oil with mint and garlic; or made into a substantial vegetarian main course, *Melanzane ripiene al sugo* (Stuffed aubergines with tomato sauce, see page 144).

These medium, round, deep-purple aubergines are typical cultivars of the Puglian region.

INVOLTINI DI MELANZANE

Aubergine (eggplant) rolls

Preparation time: 30 minutes + 30 minutes draining
Cooking time: 20 minutes
Serves 4

— 1 aubergine (eggplant),
   thinly sliced
— extra-virgin olive oil
— 100 g / 3½ oz prosciutto, cut
   into matchstick-sized pieces
— 100 g / 3½ oz mozzarella
   cheese, drained and chopped
— 1 bunch mint leaves,
   chopped, plus extra leaves
   for garnish
— salt

Arrange the aubergine (eggplant) slices on a work counter. Sprinkle with salt and let drain for 30 minutes. Rinse the aubergine, and pat dry with paper towels.

Preheat the oven to 200°C / 400°F / Gas Mark 6. Brush an oven dish with oil.

Put the prosciutto, mozzarella and chopped mint leaves into a bowl, add a drizzle of oil and a pinch of salt, then carefully mix together. Place a spoonful of the mixture at the widest end of each aubergine slice, roll up tightly and secure with cocktail sticks or toothpicks.

Place the rolls in the prepared dish and bake for 10 minutes. Garnish with mint leaves and serve.

TIMBALLO DI PASTA

Pasta timbale

This is a dish for special occasions, well worth the time it takes to make. The word *timballo* is the name of a mould, slightly unusual in having a diameter equal to its height. The food cooked in it goes by the same name as it has the same shape.

Preparation time: 1½ hours + 1 hour standing
Cooking time: 2 hours
Serves 8–10

— 3 aubergines (eggplants), peeled and sliced
— vegetable oil, for frying
— 2 eggs, beaten
— 100 g / 3 oz (1 cup) dried breadcrumbs
— 250 g / 9 oz thin penne pasta
— 150 g / 5 oz mozzarella cheese, sliced
— 50 g / 2 oz (½ cup) grated Parmesan cheese

For the meat sauce:
— 400 g / 14 oz pork slices
— salt and pepper
— 2 tablespoons grated Parmesan cheese
— 100 g / 3½ oz cured ham slices
— vegetable oil, for frying
— 100 ml / 3½ fl oz (scant ½ cup) red wine
— 800 ml / 28 fl oz (3½ cups) tomato sauce
— hot chicken stock (optional)

Salt the aubergine (eggplant) slices and leave for about 1 hour to expel their excess moisture. Rinse, drain and squeeze dry.

Heat a 2.5-cm / 1-inch depth of the oil in a sauté pan. Put the eggs and breadcrumbs in separate shallow bowls. When the oil is hot, dip some aubergine slices first in the egg, then in the breadcrumbs, and fry a few at a time until golden. Drain on paper towels.

To make the sauce, place the pork slices on a chopping (cutting) board and beat with a rolling pin or heavy-based saucepan until thin. Season them, sprinkle with 2 tablespoons Parmesan, cover with the ham slices, then roll up and secure with cocktail sticks or toothpicks.

Heat a little oil in a frying pan or skillet, add the meat rolls and brown on all sides. Drizzle the wine over them, allow to evaporate, then add the tomato sauce and simmer for 10 minutes, adding a little hot stock if the mixture seems too thick. Set aside to cool, then remove the cocktail sticks and coarsely chop the meat rolls. Return to the saucepan, cook over high heat for 5 minutes and reduce the sauce until thickened.

Meanwhile, cook the penne in a large saucepan of boiling salted water until al dente. Drain and mix with the meat sauce and 4 tablespoons of Parmesan.

To make the meatballs, put the minced veal in a bowl, add the egg yolk, cheese, salt and pepper and mix well. Shape into walnut-sized meatballs. Fry in hot oil for 5–7 minutes until they are golden brown or boil in stock for 5 minutes.

Preheat the oven to 180°C / 350°F / Gas Mark 4. Grease a 26-cm / 10-inch ring mould and place on a baking sheet.

To make the pastry, place the flour in a mound on a work counter, make a well in the centre and add the lard, sugar, egg yolks and wine. Knead until you have a smooth dough. Cut off two-thirds, place on a lightly floured counter and shape into a ball. Flatten slightly, then roll into a circle and use to line the prepared mould.

Arrange alternating layers of the pasta, aubergine, mozzarella, meatballs and remaining Parmesan in the pastry case, finishing with a layer of aubergine. Roll out the remaining pastry and use to cover the filled mould, pressing the edges firmly together. Trim off the excess, then brush the surface with a little beaten egg.

Cut a small hole in the centre of the pie and insert a 'chimney' – for example, a cannoli tube – in order to release steam during cooking. Brush again with beaten egg and bake for about 1 hour, until golden brown. When done, leave to stand for 15 minutes, then remove the ring, slide the timbale onto a plate and serve.

For the meatballs:
— 150 g / 5 oz minced (ground) veal
— 1 egg yolk
— 50 g / 2 oz (½ cup) grated Parmesan cheese
— salt and pepper
— vegetable oil or stock

For the pastry:
— 500 g / 1 lb 2 oz (4 cups) plain (all-purpose) flour, plus extra for dusting
— 200 g / 7 oz (1 cup) lard or (1¾ sticks) butter
— 50 g / 2 oz (¼ cup) sugar
— 5 egg yolks
— 4 tablespoons dry white wine

LAMB

When a region is so deeply tied to the land, the seasons
take on special significance, and nothing says 'spring'
like succulent lamb from the Gentile di Puglia breed.
Raised on the rocky ridges of the mountainous interior,
and much admired for the fineness of its wool and
the lean, grassy flavour of its meat, it goes especially
well with other seasonal treats, such as fresh peas and
cardoncelli (early cardoons).

Both Puglia and Basilicata have tended to reserve meat
for special occasions, and have a wealth of creative
dishes that make the most of it. In Bari, for example,
the most spectacular of these is *U'verdette,* an Easter
extravaganza of lamb and peas, slowly roasted until
spoon-tender, then smothered in a thick and creamy
sauce of beaten eggs, pecorino cheese and parsley.
In the hinterland a similar dish uses cardoons that grow
wild and abundant in the hedges. However, both of
these ideas evolved from an even simpler dish that
originated in Martina Franca, which is celebrated across
the region for the sweetness of its lamb, and where they
devour everything from the tongue to the tail in a
tongue-twisting dish called *Gnummerieddi.* Consisting
of chunks of rosy lamb skewered alternately with offal
(variety meats) and wrapped in a lacy caul, it is grilled
over hot embers, and scattered with pecorino shavings
and parsley before serving.

The Comisana breed
of sheep, indigenous to
Sicily, is now farmed
across Italy. The breed is
well known for producing
a plentiful supply of milk.

*Lamb with
wild fennel*

Wild fennel, commonly known as *finocchietto* in Italy, grows in fields and along roadsides all over the country. It has a very intense aroma and the seeds, particularly in the south of Italy, are widely used in many sweet and savoury dishes.

Preparation time: 45 minutes
Cooking time: 1 hour 30 minutes
Serves 6

— 1 × 1 kg / 2¼ lb shoulder
  or leg of lamb
— 1 clove garlic, halved
— 1 small onion, sliced
— 2 small tomatoes,
  roughly chopped
— 4 sprigs parsley
— 2 kg / 4½ lb wild fennel
— 200 g / 7 oz stringy fresh
  scamorza cheese, sliced
— 120 g / 4½ oz (1¼ cups)
  grated pecorino or
  Parmesan cheese
— 3 eggs
— salt and pepper

Place the lamb in a large saucepan and add a little water, the garlic, onion, tomatoes and parsley. Bring to a boil, then cover and simmer for about 1 hour, until the meat is tender. Transfer the lamb to a plate and leave to cool, reserving the cooking juices.

Cook the wild fennel in a saucepan of boiling salted water for 10 minutes, then drain.

Preheat the oven to 200°C / 400°F / Gas Mark 6.

When the lamb is cool enough to handle, bone it, season and cut into bite-sized pieces. Heat a few spoonfuls of the lamb cooking juices in a frying pan or skillet. Add the fennel and infuse for a few minutes.

Reserve 3 tablespoons of grated pecorino for the topping. Arrange alternating layers of fennel, meat, scamorza and grated cheese in a large baking dish, finishing with a layer of grated cheese. Bake in a hot oven at 200°C / 400°F / Gas Mark 6 for about 10 minutes, or until the scamorza starts to melt.

Put the eggs in a bowl, add the reserved grated cheese, season and beat well. Pour the mixture over the meat dish and bake for another 15 minutes, until the surface is well browned. Leave to stand for 5 minutes before serving.

ALEATICO WINE

During the fourteenth century, the Italian wine writer Pietro Crescenzi wrote about the extraordinary finesse of a wine being produced in southern Italy from the Livatica (now Aleatico) grape. Whether it was originally imported from Greece or a native to Puglia is unclear, but the wine certainly became a favourite of Napoleon during his exile on Elba, and has been highly rated nationally ever since, earning its own DOC (*Denominazione di Origine Controllata*) status in 1972.

It is a high-quality, red dessert wine produced all over Puglia using at least 85 per cent Aleatico grapes bolstered by Negroamaro, Primitivo and Malvasia Nera varieties, which have been left to dry slightly on the plant or on grass mats. The drying gives the wine an elegant richness: warm and sweet with floral notes, plus a subtle acidity that makes it refreshing rather than cloying. It is considered the ultimate accompaniment to regional pastries, such as delicate *mostaccioli* made from almond paste.

With high humidity and cool temperatures, wine caves are a common form of storage and ageing of wine.

ALMONDS

Puglian *mandorle* (almonds) are far from being average nuts. Sweet, smooth and milky, they are perfect for producing high-quality marzipan, and also often included in the region's famous cakes, pastries and desserts. They have been cultivated in the region for at least 7,000 years, and survive poor soil even over the winter, which makes them something of a perfect crop for frugal Pugliese.

The best almonds come from Salento, and on saints' days the piazzas of Salentine villages fill with the aroma of the nuts roasting over wood-burning fires. These are sold in paper cones for people to munch on as they take their evening stroll. However, it is when the nuts are turned into local desserts, such as *amaretti*, *rosata* (see page 52), *bocconotti* (see page 115) and *cricchognoli* (see page 78), and washed down with *orzata* (chilled, sweetened almond milk) or iced coffee mixed with almond milk that they become pure heaven.

At Christmas it is traditional for the nuns at the convent of San Giovanni Evangelista in Lecce to make a fish-shaped cake (see page 210) to celebrate the birth of Christ, who made fishers of men. It is filled with a Marsala-flavoured cream called *faldacchiera*.

Almonds grow abundantly in Italy, and the paste made from them is used to make all kinds of sweet treats, often shaped to celebrate various festivals or seasons.

ROSATA DI MANDORLE

Almond 'rosata'

Preparation time: 40 minutes
Cooking time: 30 minutes
Serves 6

— 6 eggs, separated
— 175 g / 6 oz (¾ cup
    plus 2 tablespoons)
    granulated sugar
— 50 g / 2 oz (½ cup) plain
    (all-purpose) flour, sifted
— pinch of ground cinnamon
— 4 tablespoons Strega liqueur
— 300 g / 11 oz (3 cups)
    blanched almonds
— 1 teaspoon lemon juice
— 100 g / 3½ oz (½ cup)
    chocolate chips
— icing (confectioners') sugar,
    for sprinkling
— grated chocolate, for
    sprinkling

Preheat the oven to 180°C / 350°F / Gas Mark 4.
Line a 26-cm / 10-inch baking pan with baking
(parchment) paper.

Put the egg yolks and half the granulated sugar
in a bowl, then whisk well. Add the flour, cinnamon
and liqueur and whisk again.

Put the almonds in a blender or food processor,
add the remaining granulated sugar and whiz to
a fine consistency.

Put the egg whites into a clean, grease-free bowl,
add the lemon juice and whisk into stiff peaks.
Using a wooden spoon, and always stirring in the
same direction, fold a spoonful of the whites into
the flour mixture, followed by 2 spoonfuls of
almonds. Continue in this way until all the whites
and almonds have been combined.

Pour the cake mixture into the prepared pan
and sprinkle with the chocolate chips. Bake for
about 30 minutes. Allow to cool in the pan, then
turn it out onto a plate and sprinkle with the icing
(confectioners') sugar and grated chocolate.

Soft orange tart

Preparation time: 1 hour and 30 minutes
Cooking time: 45 minutes
Serves 8–10

— 4 eggs, separated
— 200 g / 7 oz (1 cup) caster (superfine) sugar
— zest and juice of 1 orange
— 4 tablespoons olive oil
— zest of 1 lemon
— 170 g / 6 oz (1½ cups) plain (all-purpose) flour
— 15 g / ½ oz (1 tablespoon) baking powder
— 1 teaspoon lemon juice
— icing (confectioners') sugar, for dusting
— orange slices and zest, to garnish

For the pastry:
— 4 tablespoons milk
— 1 teaspoon baking powder
— 350 g / 12 oz (2¾ cups) plain (all-purpose) flour, plus extra for dusting
— 150 g / 4 oz (⅔ cup) caster (superfine) sugar
— 2 egg yolks
— 150 g / 5 oz (1 stick plus 2 tablespoons) softened butter, plus extra for greasing
— zest of 1 lemon
— pinch of salt
— marmalade, for spreading

Preheat the oven to 180°C / 350°F / Gas Mark 4. Butter and flour a 28-cm / 11-inch springform cake pan.

First make the pastry. Put the milk in a cup, add the baking powder and stir until dissolved. Place the flour in a mound on a work counter, make a well in the centre and add the baking powder liquid, sugar, egg yolks, butter, lemon zest and salt. Using your fingertips, mix together the ingredients in the well until they are combined, then gradually draw in the flour until a smooth paste is formed. Flatten into a disc and wrap in clingfilm (plastic wrap). Chill for 30 minutes. Roll into a circle large enough to line the prepared pan. Trim off the excess and prick the pastry case with a fork. Spread a little marmalade all over it and place in the refrigerator while you make the filling.

Cream the egg yolks and sugar in a bowl. Whisk in the orange juice, oil, both citrus zests, then add the flour and baking powder.

Put the egg whites and lemon juice into a clean, grease-free bowl and whisk into stiff peaks. Gently fold into the flour mixture a bit at a time. Pour into the pastry case and bake for about 45 minutes. (Cover with baking [parchment] paper after 30 minutes if it is browning too quickly.) Bake until well risen and golden brown and the top springs back when lightly pressed with a finger. Cool the tart in the pan, then transfer to a plate. Trim any excess pastry using a sharp knife. Sprinkle the tart with the icing (confectioners') sugar and garnish with the zest and orange slices.

II

BARLETTA-ANDRIA-TRANI

Pure di fave e cicorielle 65
Broad (fava) bean and wild chicory purée

Cavatelli e broccoletti 68
Cavatelli with broccoli

Pollo ripieno 70
Stuffed chicken

Tegame di calamari e patate al forno 73
Baked squid and potatoes

Cartellate 76
Honey pastry flowers

Cricchognoli di bisceglie 78
Chocolate almond biscuits

BARLETTA-ANDRIA-TRANI

The area encompassing Barletta, Andria and Trani was established as a province in its own right in 2009, so you might be forgiven for not having heard of it. This is Puglia's smallest and least populous province, of which the capital is Barletta. A small but handsome town overlooking the Adriatic, it rests in a rich and hilly landscape, with thick areas of woodland that almost burst into flame with the changing colours of autumn. Perhaps inevitably, it still relies largely on agriculture for its economy, and the land is sewn together by an intricate network of canals that separate neatly planted fields of organic vegetables, salad leaves (greens), tomatoes, cucumbers and aubergines (eggplants), as well as dense fruit orchards, all of them watched over by crumbling medieval castles.

Bordered by Margherita di Saviola to the north, Bisceglie to the south and extending inland as far as Spinazzola, the region has a burgeoning number of marvellously off-the-beaten-path 'agriturismo' properties, where visitors can stay on local farms and enjoy some of the best and most authentic food experiences in the country. Many of the ingredients are grown or reared locally – indeed, the Alta Murgia National Park in the heart of the region is revered not just for its scenic walks, but for the quality of the lamb that is raised there. This means that local cuisine is as slow as slow food gets.

Andria has two claims to fame. The first is the Castel del Monte, an imposing Swabian structure built by Federico II as a hunting lodge and declared a World Heritage Site in 1996; it appears on the reverse side of the Italian one euro coin. The second is the celebrated burrata cheese (see page 67), made from the snowy white milk of water buffalo. It is traditionally wrapped in asphodel leaves, their greenness affirming the freshness of the cheese within, as it turns after 48 hours. For that reason, its availability outside Andria is

Page 56:
Durum wheat is the mainstay of Puglian cuisine. It has a much higher gluten content than regular wheat and forms the basis of Puglian pastas and breads.

Trani port was one of the most important and prosperous trading ports of Italy in medieval times.

a relatively recent phenomenon, and to this day it is often made fresh, right in front of you, in local restaurants, and paired with local red wines such as Nero de Troia and Bombino.

The coast, like everywhere else in the region, feels like a well-kept secret: it's quiet and tranquil, with some lovely beaches, such as that at Bisceglie. But it is Trani that seduces food and wine lovers, with its delightful, horseshoe-shaped port filled with superb fish restaurants that look north to the limestone cathedral winking in the sun. Between the eleventh and thirteenth centuries the city was also home to the biggest Jewish community in southern Italy, which naturally affected the cuisine. In an essay about the Jewish cooking of Italy, the American-Italian chef Walter Potenza described a salad 'of field greens with a condiment of tomatoes, seedless cucumbers and a vinaigrette of pomegranate juice and walnuts' from the Trani Jewish quarter.

Among the highly regarded local wines is Moscato di Trani, a DOC dessert wine produced in a handful of areas between the provinces of Bari and Foggia from white Moscato grapes, which are left to dry on the plant until mid-October. The style of this wine ranges from sweet and light – perfect for easy drinking – to velvety with hints of moss and almond, ideal for serving with dry pastries and full-flavoured cheeses. Thanks to its leanness, better-quality Moscato is excellent for sipping, leaving the drinker with no cloying aftertaste.

A colourful array of seafood at a fish market. The extensive coastline means the Pugliese are spoilt for choice.

Pages 74–5:
Dappled sunlight filters through an olive tree. Puglia is home to a number of renowned cultivars, including the Coratino olive.

WILD CHICORY

Chicory (endive), especially field or wild chicory, is something of a cult vegetable in the South. Best foraged in the autumn or spring, the new-growth young leaves and the pretty, cornflower blue flowers can be eaten raw in a salad, but the Pugliese prefer the bitter leaves (greens) boiled and served as an integral part of one of the region's oldest, most traditional and much beloved dishes, *Pure di fave e cicorielle* (Broad [fava] bean and wild chicory purée, see page 65). Housewives in Basilicata who, when tackling the difficult task of producing both lunch and dinner, succeeded in making even this most humble of ingredients, appetizing. The broad (fava) beans are soaked for a whole day and are then boiled over a low heat until they are reduced to a purée. Meanwhile, the chicory (preferably the wild kind) is boiled with salt and drained.

According to tradition the dish is presented with the purée on one side and the vegetables on the other (the ingredients are probably kept separate to give an impression of abundance) although these days the purée is spread over a dish with a large amount of the robust local extra-virgin olive oil, the pride of the region, swirled over the top and the chicory leaves piled on top.

Vibrant wild chicory ready for market. Boiling the chicory and discarding the liquid reduces the bitterness of the leaves.

PURE DI FAVE E CICORIELLE

While this is one of the most popular vegetable-based dishes in Puglia, a very similar dish called *fave e foglie* (beans and leaves) is cooked throughout southern Italy. In that case, however, just the beans are pureed and the vegetables are used as garnish.

Broad (fava) bean and wild chicory purée

Preparation time: 25 minutes + 12 hours soaking
Cooking time: 3 hour 30 minutes
Serves 6

Drain the beans, then put them in a saucepan of water and bring to a boil. Cover and simmer for about 3 hours, until very soft. Push the beans through a sieve (strainer), discarding the skins, and set aside the purée.

Put the wild chicory into a saucepan of boiling salted water and cook for 1–2 minutes, until tender. Drain and chop coarsely.

Heat the oil in a frying pan or skillet. When hot, add the garlic clove and fry until brown. Discard the garlic, then add the wild chicory and stir for a minute or so to flavour it with the oil.

Heat the bean purée, then add salt to taste. Stir in the onion, celery, tomatoes and parsley. Transfer to a serving dish, top with wild chicory, drizzle with oil and sprinkle with freshly ground pepper.

— 1 kg / 2¼ lb (2⅔ cups) dried broad (fava) beans, soaked in water for 12 hours
— 3 kg / 6 lb 8 oz wild chicory leaves
— 2 tablespoons extra-virgin olive oil, plus extra to drizzle
— 1 clove garlic
— 1 onion, chopped
— 1 celery stalk, chopped
— 2 tomatoes, skinned and seeded
— ½ bunch parsley, chopped
— salt and pepper

BURRATA

If olive oil is Puglia's 'liquid gold', milk is its 'white gold' – the essential ingredient in one of the region's most diverse products: cheese. From the smoky fagottini of Foggia to the nutty caciocavallo stretched curd cheese (see page 224) of the Apennine Mountains and the intensely flavoured sheep's milk cacioricotta of Salento, Puglia's cheeses are wildly varied. In terms of sheer decadence, though, there is one that outshines all others: the legendary burrata of Andria.

A relatively recent invention, created in the 1920s by Lorenzo Bianchino Chieppa on his farm in the tiny municipality of Piana Padula, burrata (literally 'buttery') has a meltingly tender outer casing of mozzarella containing an oozing heart of very fresh cream. Although rich, it has a curiously cleansing, faintly acidic taste, and quickly became much in demand among Puglian gourmands. Since then, the popularity of burrata has spread throughout Italy, and now extends to the rest of Europe and the United States.

It is best enjoyed as fresh and cool as possible, and Puglian *osterias* often serve it as a simple but stylish salad dotted with vine-ripened tomatoes and olives. On the other hand, it can also be served to begin an extravagant meal drizzled with high-grade truffle oil and freshly ground black pepper.

An invention of the early twentieth century, burrata is best served with a drizzle of high-quality olive oil and freshly ground pepper.

*Cavatelli
with broccoli*

The little curls of pasta known as *cavatelli*, or *cavatieddi* in the Puglian dialect, are very common in southern Italy, where they are often home-made, but also produced industrially. They tend to be served very simply, as in the recipe below. You could also try them with a sauce of tomatoes, rocket (arugula) and pecorino, or with oil, chopped garlic and anchovies.

Preparation time: 50 minutes
Cooking time: 40 minutes
Serves 6

— 800 g / 1¾ lb (8 cups)
   broccoli, separated into
   small florets
— extra-virgin olive oil,
   for drizzling
— salt and pepper
— grated Parmesan,
   for sprinkling

For the pasta:
— 1 kg / 2¼ lb (8 cups)
   '00' flour
— 2 tablespoons olive oil
— salt

For the pasta, place the flour in a mound on a work counter, make a well in the centre and add a pinch of salt, the oil and just enough water to form a firm dough. Take a small piece of dough at a time and roll into a long cylinder about 1 cm / ½ inch thick. Slice the cylinder into 2-cm / ¾-inch long pieces. Roll each piece into a little cylinder. Place the back of a knife along the edge of a cylinder and push it down and away from you so that the pasta curls around it. Repeat with the remaining dough.

Cook the pasta and broccoli in large, separate saucepans of boiling salted water until al dente. Drain and place both in a bowl. Drizzle with oil, season and stir well. Sprinkle with Parmesan and serve immediately.

POLLO RIPIENO

Stuffed chicken

Preparation time: 15 minutes
Cooking time: 1 hour 30 minutes + 15 minutes resting
Serves 4

— 1 x 1.5-kg (3 lb 5-oz) chicken
   with giblets, plus
   2 extra chicken livers
— 100 g / 3½ oz dry-cured ham
— 3 slices crustless bread,
   soaked in water
— 25 g / 1 oz (¼ cup) grated
   Parmesan cheese
— 1 egg, lightly beaten
— 2 sprigs rosemary, plus extra
   for garnish
— 4 sage leaves
— 2 tablespoons melted butter
— 3 tablespoons olive oil
— salt and pepper

Preheat the oven to 180°C / 350°F / Gas Mark 4.

Season the chicken cavity. Chop the giblets, extra livers
and ham and put them into a bowl. Squeeze out the
bread and add to the giblet mixture, along with
the cheese and egg and season. Mix well.

Spoon the stuffing into the chicken, then close the
opening with a wooden cocktail stick or toothpick.
Lift the wings and slip a sprig of rosemary and a couple
of sage leaves underneath them. Put the bird into
a roasting pan, brush it with butter and oil, and sprinkle
with salt. Roast for about 1½ hours, basting several
times, until golden brown. It's ready if the juices
run clear when a skewer or the tip of a sharp knife
is inserted into the thickest part of the leg.

Allow the chicken to rest for 15 minutes, then sprinkle
with rosemary leaves. Carve the chicken and arrange
the meat on a serving dish. Spoon the stuffing around
it and serve.

TEGAME DI CALAMARI
E PATATE AL FORNO

Although delicious made with squid, this recipe can also be made with cuttlefish, which has a similar appearance. The main difference is that the cuttlefish has a hard backbone called the 'cuttlebone', while squid has a cartilage tube, known as the 'quill'.

Preparation time: 20 minutes
Cooking time: 30–40 minutes
Serves 6–8

Preheat the oven to 200°C / 400°F / Gas Mark 6.

To make the stuffing, put the breadcrumbs into a bowl with the cheese, egg, parsley and seasoning. Mix well, then spoon the stuffing into the cavities of the squid and secure each one with a wooden cocktail stick or toothpick.

Pour the oil into an oven dish, then arrange the onion, garlic and half the tomatoes on top. Sprinkle with a tablespoon of the parsley and some salt. Sit the squid on top, arrange the potato wedges around the edge of the pan, and then add the remaining tomatoes and parsley. Season and bake for about 30–40 minutes, until potatoes are tender. Allow to stand for a few minutes before serving.

*Baked squid
and potatoes*

— 1 kg / 2¼ lb squid, cleaned
— 2 tablespoons olive oil
— 1 small onion, sliced
— 1 clove garlic, chopped
— 5 ripe tomatoes, skinned
  and chopped
— 2 tablespoons chopped
  parsley
— 500 g / 1 lb 2 oz potatoes,
  peeled and cut into wedges
— salt and pepper

For the stuffing:
— 200 g / 7 oz (2 cups) fresh
  crustless breadcrumbs
— 65 g / 2½ oz (¾ cup) grated
  Parmesan or pecorino cheese
— 1 egg
— 6 tablespoons chopped
  parsley
— salt and pepper

CARTELLATE

Honey pastry flowers

Preparation time: 40 minutes + 4 hours rising
Cooking time: 30 minutes
Makes 8 large or 16 small pastries

— 500 g / 1 lb 2 oz (4 cups) plain
   (all-purpose) flour, plus extra
   for dusting
— salt
— 7 g / ¼ oz (2¼ teaspoons)
   easy blend (quick rise) yeast
— 100 ml / 3½ fl oz (scant ½ cup)
   olive oil
— 100 ml / 3½ fl oz (scant ½ cup)
   white wine
— vegetable oil, for deep-frying
— 350 g / 12 oz (1½ cups) honey
— sprinkles, for decorating

Place the flour in a mound on a work counter, make
a well in the centre and add a pinch of salt, the yeast,
oil, wine and 120 ml / 4 fl oz (½ cup) lukewarm water.
Quickly work in the flour until you have a soft, not
sticky, dough. Knead for 5–10 minutes, until the dough
is smooth. Cover with clingfilm (plastic wrap) and
leave in a warm place to rise for 2 hours, or until
doubled in size.

Divide the dough into 8 equal pieces, place them on a
lightly floured surface and roll into balls. Using a rolling
pin, roll them into very thin rounds with a diameter of
25–30 cm / 10–12 inches. Using a pastry wheel, cut each
round into a long spiral strip about 5 cm / 2 inches wide.

Fold each strip in half lengthways and roll into a loose
spiral. The finished spiral should look roughly like a
rose. Set aside at room temperature for 2 hours.

Heat a one-third depth of oil in a large saucepan. It's
hot enough when a cube of bread browns in 20 seconds
(180°C / 375°F). Carefully deep-fry the pastries one at
a time for about 2 minutes each, or until golden brown,
turning over halfway through the cooking time. Scoop
out with a slotted spoon and drain them upside down
on paper towels.

Heat the honey in a small saucepan. Using tongs,
quickly dip the pastries in it, then arrange them on
a platter and drizzle over more honey, if desired.
Decorate with sprinkles and serve warm.

CRICCHIGNOLI DI BISCEGLIE

*Chocolate
almond biscuits*

Preparation time: 20 minutes
Cooking time: 20 minutes
Makes 18

— 200 g / 7 oz (1½ cups)
unblanched almonds
— 250 g / 9 oz (1¼ cups) caster
(superfine) sugar
— 1 tablespoon unsweetened
cocoa powder
— zest of 1 lemon
— 3 egg whites
— 1 teaspoon lemon juice

Preheat the oven to 150°C / 300°F / Gas Mark 2.
Line a baking sheet with baking (parchment) paper.

Roughly chop the almonds, then mix with 200 g / 7 oz
(1 cup) of the sugar, cocoa powder and lemon zest.

Whip 2 of the egg whites to stiff peaks with the lemon
juice and carefully fold into the almond mixture.

Dip your fingers in the bowl and, taking a little mixture
at a time, mould into small rounds on to the baking
sheet. Beat the remaining egg white, lightly brush
the top of each biscuit (cookies) and sprinkle with
the remaining sugar.

Bake for about 20 minutes. Remove from the oven
and cool on a wire rack before serving. Store in an
airtight container.

III

BARI

BARI

Page 80:
Polignano a Mare,
or Polignano at Sea,
is a beautiful town
that sits on a cliff over
looking the Adriatic Sea.

Occupying a lofty position overlooking the Adriatic
Sea, Puglia's capital Bari is second only to Naples
in terms of its strategic importance as a port. Indeed,
it was once an important Roman settlement, serving
as a useful junction between the coast road and the via
Traiana, which connected the peninsula with the east.

Its population has grown to nearly one million
in recent times, and the city is now increasingly
cosmopolitan. To the north, the ancient Bari Vecchia
(old town) is a complicated knot of narrow streets
and shadowy alleyways that once had a reputation
as the underbelly of the region. Following a recent
regeneration programme, it has turned into an
atmospheric hub for bars and restaurants centred
around the piazzas Mercantile and Ferrarese. It is also
home to several important monuments, including
the Basilica of St Nicholas, which houses the relics
of the saint in the crypt, and from which Peter the
Hermit preached the importance of launching the first
Crusade to retake the holy city of Jerusalem from the
Saracens. Consequently, Bari has been an important
pilgrimage site since the eleventh century, and present-
day visitors still come from far and wide. Among the
sites of special interest is the mighty Castello Svevo,
a walled city within the walled city, that was restored
by Emperor Federico II in 1233, whose interest
in food also did much to cement Puglia's reputation
as a gastronomic heavyweight.

The Murattiano district to the south of Bari was built
in the early nineteenth century by Joachim Murat,
Napoleon's brother-in-law, who was brought in to
improve living conditions following a malaria epidemic
that lasted for generations. It is an impressive feat of
modern town planning, laid out on a practical grid
system and bordered by an elegant seafront boulevard
book-ended by two ports – the old and the new – with
the smart shopping districts of the via Sparano and via

Archaeologists discovered
that Bitonto Cathedral,
the largest cathedral in
Puglia, had been built
on top of a church dating
from the fifth century.

Argiro unfurling along it. In Roman times the old harbour had been an important fishery, both for the day's catch and for the creation of fermented fish sauce, an essential condiment known as *garum*. In Medieval times the port developed into an important trading post for slaves, who became known as 'white gold'. They were mainly Slavic, and destined for Muslim states surrounding the Mediterranean, such as Tunisia, Morocco, Sicily and Córdoba. Since those days, Murattiano too has smartened up its act, with stylish bars and restaurants just a short stroll from its blue-painted fishing craft. Despite the change of emphasis, the seafood market still provides a window into traditional Baresi life. Get there early enough and you will find local fishermen selling the city's speciality of raw seafood, including tiny pink prawns (shrimp), tender mussels, freshly opened sea urchins or slices of raw octopus. All these delicacies are usually accompanied by refreshing cold beer.

Beyond the city limits, Bari is the fifth largest province in Italy, fondly nicknamed the 'California of the South' for its climate, terroir and coast. The Murge Plateau offers seemingly endless panoramas forming a patchwork of wheat fields that produce the grain used to make the region's celebrated Altamura bread and *orecchiette* pasta. The landscape is also dotted with dramatic limestone formations and deep ravines, scattered liberally with olive and almond groves, the former producing Terra de Bari PDO olive oil, which is second to none. Then there are multiple terraces of neat vineyards with their sprawling *masserie* (ancient farmhouses) that doubled as fortresses during the region's various sieges.

A typical Puglian deli will stock pasta, olive oil, cheese and delicious dry-cured meats.

The Itria valley is famous for the toadstool-like *trulli*, whitewashed houses with slate-grey conical roofs, garlanded in late summer with the red peppers that flavour so many of the region's dishes. The white sandy beaches of the coast stretch from Molfetta, north of Bari, to Monopoli in the south, and are dotted with picture-perfect fishing villages, such as Giovinazzo and Polignano a Mare, the latter notable for its arc of golden sand flanked by steep limestone cliffs from which many caves and inlets have been hewn, including the legendary Grotto Palazzese. It all invites lazy days spent ambling about, stopping for a dip in the turquoise sea and feasting on fish and seafood hauled from the water just moments before.

An old church in the town of Monopoli sits on the coast of the Adriatic.

Pages 87–8:
Bari's landscape is dotted with limestone cliffs and the town of Polignano a Mare is a popular destination for cliff divers.

PEPERONI VERDI RIPIENI E FRITTI

Peppers are a good source of vitamin C and have the advantage of being very low in calories. This tasty and full-flavoured dish is ideal during the summer thanks to its blend of Mediterranean flavours.

Stuffed and fried green peppers

Preparation time: 30 minutes
Cooking time: 30 minutes
Serves 6

To make the stuffing, put the breadcrumbs in a bowl with the cheeses, eggs, parsley, garlic and capers. Season and mix well.

Cut the cap off the peppers, remove the seeds with a teaspoon and spoon the stuffing into the cavities. Heat the oil in a frying pan or skillet, add the peppers and fry until lightly browned on all sides. Lift out with a slotted spoon and drain on paper towels.

Discard any excess oil in the pan, then add the tomatoes and cook over a high heat for 10 minutes to reduce their liquid. Add the peppers to the sauce and simmer gently for 5–10 minutes. Transfer to a serving dish and serve.

— 6 pointed green
  (sweet) peppers
— vegetable oil, for frying
— 500 g / 1 lb 2 oz (2¾ cups)
  canned chopped tomatoes

For the stuffing:
— 50 g / 2 oz (½ cup) dry
  crustless breadcrumbs
— 2 tablespoons grated
  Parmesan cheese
— 1 tablespoon grated
  pecorino cheese
— 1–2 eggs
— 1 teaspoon chopped parsley
— 1 clove garlic, chopped
— 1 tablespoon chopped capers
— salt and pepper

Macaroni with green beans

Preparation time: 20 minutes
Cooking time: 30 minutes
Serves 4

— olive oil, for frying
— 2 onions, finely sliced
— 2 cloves garlic, finely chopped
— 1–2 red chillies, finely sliced
— 400 g / 14 oz macaroni
— 400 g / 14 oz (7½ cups)
  French (green) beans,
  trimmed and halved
— sea salt and pepper

To serve (optional):
— extra-virgin olive oil
— grated Parmesan cheese

Heat a frying pan or skillet, add a little olive oil and slowly cook the onions for 20 minutes, until they are soft, sweet and a little browned. Add the garlic and chillies and cook for another 5 minutes.

Meanwhile, cook the pasta in a large saucepan of boiling salted water for 6–8 minutes until al dente. Add the beans and cook for another 2 minutes.

Drain the pasta, reserving a cupful of the cooking water. Add the pasta and beans to the onion pan and stir well, adding a little of the reserved water to loosen the mixture and make a sauce. Season to taste.

Finish the dish with a little grated Parmesan and a drizzle of good olive oil, if you like.

BACCALÀ (SALT COD)

Although the fifteenth-century Italian explorer John Cabot was familiar with salt cod, having encountered it on his travels, it was actually the Spanish who introduced it to southern Italy. The dried fish was much appreciated, especially inland, where storing fresh fish was almost impossible.

Traditionally, Catholics abstained from eating meat on Fridays and *baccalà* was often prepared throughout the winter months, poached in milk and garnished with boiled eggs and olives. Inevitably, though, Puglia and Basilicata have devised many imaginative ways to use this most simple of ingredients. Yet the dish most typical of the region is *Torta della vigilia di Natale* (Christmas Eve pie, see page 96), which combines flaked salt cod with bitter escarole (curly escarole or endive), earthy cauliflower and olives, sweetened with raisins and wine, while the Salento dish, *Baccalà alla salentina*, sprinkles snow-white, desalinated fish filets with breadcrumbs, pecorino cheese and fresh tomato, and bakes them with potatoes until crisp and golden.

A variety of preserved, salted fish for sale, including cod and anchovies.

TORTA DELLA VIGILIA DI NATALE

Christmas Eve pie

Preparation time: 1 hour 15 minutes, plus 4 days
soaking and 1 hour resting
Cooking time: 1 hour
Serves 8–10

— 500 g / 1 lb 2 oz dried salt cod,
  soaked in several changes
  of cold water for 4 days
— 2–3 tablespoons raisins
  (optional), soaked in warm
  water
— 500 g / 1 lb 2 oz (5 cups)
  cauliflower florets, sliced
— 500 g / 1 lb 2 oz escarole (curly
  endive or chicory), shredded
— 2 tablespoons oil, plus extra
  for greasing
— 3 onions, very thinly sliced
— 100 g / 3½ oz (1 cup) black or
  green olives, stoned (pitted)
  and chopped
— 1 sprig parsley, chopped
— salt

For the pastry:
— 500 g / 1 lb 2 oz (4 cups) plain
  (all-purpose) flour, plus extra
  for kneading
— 150 ml / 5 fl oz (⅔ cup)
  white wine
— 3 tablespoons olive oil
— ½ teaspoon salt

To make the pastry, put the flour in a bowl, make
a well in the centre and add the wine, oil and salt.
Mix with your hands until a dough forms, then knead
on a lightly floured work surface, about 5 minutes,
to form a smooth dough. Flatten into a disc, brush
with oil, wrap in clingfilm (plastic wrap) and allow
to rest at room temperature for about 1 hour.

Put the rehydrated salt cod into a saucepan of clean
water, bring to a boil and boil for about 15 minutes.
Drain and set aside. Discard the skin.

Drain the raisins and dry. Cook the cauliflower in
boiling salted water for about 5 minutes, or until
tender. Refresh under cold water and drain. Blanch
the escarole (curly endive or chicory) in a pan
of boiling water for 2 minutes. Drain and set aside.

Heat the oil in a small frying pan or skillet, cook
the onions until soft and translucent. Set aside.

Flake the salt cod in a bowl, add the raisins, onions,
cauliflower, escarole, olives and parsley. Mix well,
season and set aside.

Preheat the oven to 190°C / 375°F / Gas Mark 5.
Oil a 30-cm / 12-inch oven dish. Cut off two-thirds
of the dough, roll out thinly and line the prepared
dish. Tip the filling into the pastry case. Roll out the
remaining dough and use to cover the filling. Trim off
the excess, crimp the edges to seal. Bake for 30 minutes,
until the pastry is golden. Serve either warm or cold.

ORECCHIETTE

The workhorse of southern Italian home cooking
is undoubtedly *orecchiette* (little ears) pasta, sometimes
called *recchiètedde* in Bari and *cappello del prete* (priest's
cap) elsewhere. The various names come from the shape
of the pasta, which evolved from a type of gnocchi
known as *cavatieddi* (see page 68). Both use the same
type of dough, and until a few years ago were still sold
by women sitting in the doorway of their homes in old
Bari to supplement the family income. It remains a
point of pride among present-day home cooks to make
the pasta by hand using one part semolina to two parts
white flour mixed with spring water. The pieces of
dough are then dragged over wood to form coin-sized
discs and shaped into 'ears' with a quick flick of the
thumb. The texture of the wood creates the fine ridges
that allow sauces to cling to them so well.

They can be served with horsemeat *ragú* or gossamer-
thin strips of lardo and sun-dried tomatoes combined
with olive oil, chillies and oregano, then sprinkled
with very dry ricotta. The classic accompaniment,
though, is tender stems of slightly bitter broccoli rabe
(see page 103) combined with salted anchovies
(*Orecchiette* with broccoli rabe, see page 104). In case you
doubt the importance of *orecchiette* in southern Italy, the
church of San Nicola still holds a sixteenth-century
deed in which a proud father bequeathed his daughter a
bakery in recognition of her skills as an orecchiette-
maker.

Women line the streets
of Bari making *orecchiette*
by hand on wooden tables
dusted with semolina.

Pages 100–1:
The method of making
orecchiette is passed down
through generations. Once
the 'little ears' are formed
they are left to dry on wire
mesh screens.

BROCCOLI RABE

If Puglia had a national vegetable, it would surely be *cime di rapa*, known as broccoli rabe in English. This hardy plant is a member of the mustard family, with wide, frilly leaves and yellow buds and flowers that burst into life in early spring. It has a distinctively nutty and pleasantly bitter flavour that has long been used for giving a kick to the region's humbler dishes. It can, for example, simply be sautéed with fried bread, or stewed with garlic, oil and pepper, but the most iconic dish is made by combining the tenderest shoots with *orecchiette* pasta (see page 98), some robust salted anchovies and lavish amounts of fruity green olive oil. The sauce clings to every ridge and furrow of the pasta, making for a hearty dish that provides optimum nourishment and maximum flavour – a true monument of regional Mediterranean cuisine.

Vivid green broccoli rabe on sale at a Puglian market. It is an excellent source of vitamins C and K.

ORECCHIETTE CON CIME DI RAPA

Orecchiette with broccoli rabe

There is no documentary proof of *orecchiette* originating in Puglia. The early historian Varrone, a native of Rome, talks of *lixulae*, a type of round pasta with a concave centre. The Pugliese merely say that the shape of *orecchiette* is that of *trulli*, the traditional conical huts of the region.

Preparation time: 1 hour + 1 hour drying
Cooking time: 25 minutes
Serves 6

— 200 g / 7 oz (1¼ cups) semolina flour
— 400 g / 14 oz (3¼ cups) '00' flour, plus extra for dusting
— pinch of salt
— grated Parmesan, to serve

For the sauce:
— 1 kg / 2¼ lb broccoli rabe
— 100 ml / 3½ fl oz (scant ½ cup) olive oil
— 1 small red chilli, seeded and sliced
— 2 cloves garlic, finely sliced
— 4–5 anchovy fillets
— salt and pepper

Mix the two types of flour in a bowl. Make a well in the centre, then add a pinch of salt and enough lukewarm water to form a smooth, dense dough. Place on a lightly floured surface and cut the dough into 8 equal pieces. Roll each piece into a cylinder about 2.5 cm / 1 inch in diameter and cover with a cloth. Slice one cylinder at a time into rounds about 5 mm / ¼ inch thick. Place the back of a knife on the edge of a round and push the dough towards you so that it curls around the blade. When you have rolled all the rounds in this way, stretch each of them over the end of your thumb to make the shape of a little ear. Continue until the dough is used up. Set aside to dry for about 1 hour. Cook the *orecchiette* in a large saucepan of salted boiling water for 2–3 minutes, until al dente. Drain and set aside.

Blanch the broccoli rabe in salted boiling water for 1 minute, then drain well. Heat some of the oil in a skillet or frying pan, add the broccoli rabe and fry for 2–3 minutes, until cooked through. Season well. Heat the remaining oil in a separate frying pan or skillet, add half the chilli and fry for 1–2 minutes, until softened. Add the garlic and fry until fragrant. Stir in the anchovies, breaking them up. Add the cooked *orecchiette* and broccoli rabe and stir well. Season to taste. Transfer to a serving dish and serve with Parmesan.

TIELLA DI RISO E COZZE

*Rice and
mussel tiella*

There are many versions of *tiella*, which is the name
of the vessel in which it is made. The dish is traditionally
baked with the mussels in the half shell, but they can
be removed prior to baking, if desired.

Preparation time: 35 minutes
Cooking time: 40 minutes + 20 minutes standing
Serves 4

— 150 ml / 5 fl oz (⅔ cup)
  vegetable oil
— 500 g / 1 lb 2 oz mussels
— 1 onion, thinly sliced
— 400 g / 14 oz (2¼ cups)
  chopped tomatoes
— 2 tablespoons chopped
  parsley
— 1 clove garlic, chopped
— 25 g / 1 oz (¼ cup) grated
  pecorino cheese
— 25 g / 1 oz (¼ cup) grated
  Parmesan cheese
— 750 g / 1 lb 8 oz potatoes,
  thinly sliced
— 150 g / 5 oz (¾ cup)
  Arborio rice
— salt and pepper

Preheat the oven to 200°C / 400°F / Gas Mark 6.
Brush a flameproof oven dish with plenty of the oil
and set aside.

Rinse and brush the mussels under running water.
Open them with a small knife, discarding the top half
of the shells.

Arrange the onion in the prepared dish and sprinkle
with half the tomatoes, a little of the parsley and garlic,
followed by half the pecorino, Parmesan and potatoes.
Place the mussels on top and cover with the rice.
Sprinkle with the remaining potatoes, cheese and
tomatoes and in that order. Drizzle the surface with
the remaining oil, season, then add enough water to
come halfway up the dish.

Place the dish over the heat and bring to the boil,
then transfer to the oven for about 40 minutes until
the rice is tender and the tiella is brown and bubbling.
Leave to rest for at least 20 minutes before serving.

OCTOPUS

The town of Fasano, situated right at the top of Italy's stiletto heel, is where its plains strewn with olive trees meet the clear blue waters of the Adriatic Sea. It is here also that the region's finest octopus is caught, especially during the early spring and summer when it comes closer to shore to hunt. A classic and very simple dish from the town is *Polpi in umido* (Stewed octopus, see page 111).

Traditionally, large octopus were beaten against the rocks to tenderize them before cooking, and local fishermen swear to this day that you do not need to add any extra water when cooking them as they will exude enough moisture to become as tender as butter. After that, the skin is rubbed off and the pinkish-purple legs are sliced and simmered for 15 minutes with aromatic ingredients, such as garlic, wild fennel, coriander (cilantro) leaves, tomatoes, wine and vinegar. Cooked like this, octopus makes for a spectacularly bright-tasting antipasti during the summer, but practical southern cooks also found a way of enjoying it through the winter too: layered in glass jars with mint leaves and garlic, then covered in wine vinegar, allowing it to keep for several months.

In August, Mola di Bari hosts *Sagra del Polpo* (Festival of octopus), where octopus is grilled over hot coals, stewed and even put into sandwiches.

POLPI IN UMIDO

Preparation time: 30 minutes
Cooking time: 1 hour 10 minutes
Serves 4

Stewed octopus

Wash the octopus under running water and cut into bite-sized pieces. Heat the oil in a flameproof casserole dish, add the garlic and fry until brown. Discard the garlic, then add the octopus and fry for a few minutes to flavour it. Pour in the wine and heat until it has evaporated.

Add the tomatoes, anchovies and seasoning to the pan. Cover and simmer for about 1 hour, until the sauce has thickened and the octopus is tender.

Transfer to a serving dish, sprinkle with the chopped parsley and serve.

— 800 g / 1¾ lb small octopus, cleaned, eyes and mouth removed
— 3 tablespoons olive oil
— 1 clove garlic
— 3 tablespoons white wine
— 350 g / 12 oz (1½ cups) canned chopped tomatoes
— 2 anchovy fillets, finely chopped
— 1 sprig parsley, chopped
— salt and pepper

BOCCONOTTI

Known as 'ladies kisses' in English, *bocconotti* were first made in Abruzzo in central Italy soon after the arrival of cocoa beans in the early 1800s. Chocolate and, indeed, anything else associated with it – such as these tender biscuits (cookies) wrapped around a mixture of chocolate, almonds and cinnamon – were strictly the preserve of the nobility until the early twentieth century, when word of these delicious mouthfuls began to spread through the masses.

The dainty little morsels were then enthusiastically adopted everywhere, with as many different regional interpretations as there were cooks who made them. Those from Sannicandro (see page 115) are the Puglian version, and make excellent use of two important regional ingredients – almonds and lemons. Unlike the northern version, these southern ones are combined with stiffly beaten egg whites, making the finished product as light as air. They are then drenched with Amaretto or Limoncello (almond or lemon liqueur). In Bari a further variation is to cut off the top and stuff the middle with sour cherry jam and cream, making an irresistible after-dinner treat.

Molfetta town lies on the coast of the Adriatic Sea. Beautiful architecture with stone details can be found among its narrow streets.

BOCCONOTTI DI SANNICANDRO

Almond cakes

This is just one of the many recipes for *bocconotti*, which are little cakes quite common in Puglia and made in different ways. Those from Bari, for example, are filled with cream and sour cherry jam. The recipe below, from Sannicandro, a village in the Gargano National Park, uses almonds and lemons.

Preparation time: 40 minutes
Cooking time: 30 minutes
Makes 24

Preheat the oven to 160°C / 325°F / Gas Mark 3.
Line 2 × 12-hole muffin pans with paper cases.

Put the egg whites and lemon juice into a bowl and whisk to stiff peaks. Blend in 200 g / 7 oz (1 cup) of the sugar.

Put the almonds and remaining sugar in another bowl and mix in the whole eggs and the lemon zest. Beat in the liqueur a little at a time. Fold the whisked egg whites into the almond mixture in 3 batches, then divide among the paper cases, filling them only two-thirds full. Bake for about 30 minutes, until golden and springy to the touch. Serve warm or at room temperature and sprinkled with icing (confectioners') sugar. Store in an airtight container.

— 5 egg whites
— ½ teaspoon lemon juice
— 300 g / 10 oz (1½ cups) caster (superfine) sugar
— 500 g / 1lb 2oz (5 cups) peeled and finely chopped almonds
— 3 eggs
— zest of 1 lemon
— 2 tablespoons Amaretto liqueur
— icing (confectioners') sugar, to serve

IV

TARANTO

TARANTO

Founded as a Greek colony in 706 BC, Taranto was among the most powerful towns in Magna Graecia. It has flourished ever since, both as a military and commercial outpost, thanks to its unique topography, which earned it the nickname 'City of Two Seas'. Jutting out on a spit of land, it separates the Mar Grande (Big Sea), which serves as a naval base, from the Mar Piccolo (Little Sea) – really more of a lagoon – which is the country's leading provider of mussels (see page 126). A less well known, though no less delicious, product of these waters is *tarantello* – tuna belly that has been salt-cured and hung in the sun to dry. Deep garnet red when ready to eat, it is sliced wafer thin, drizzled with olive oil and served with toasted almonds as an antipasto. It goes extremely well with a glass of locally made, very young Martina Bianco wine.

Although Taranto has been heavily industrialized over the years, and has well-established foundries and shipyards to show for it, the city retains a solidly handsome air. It is dominated by the Castello Aragonese, which was built in the fifteenth century to protect the city from frequent raids by Turkish corsairs. Nowadays, it forms the nucleus of the old city, which was separated from the mainland when a canal connecting the two seas was built at the end of the nineteenth century. Perched on this man-made island, Taranto is a warren of narrow streets with lively fish markets and superb seafood restaurants that are connected to, but endearingly separated from, the new town by a famous swing-bridge, the Ponte Girevole, leading to a rather grand waterside promenade known as the Vittorio Emanuelle III.

Page 116:
The Mediterranean climate provides the perfect conditions for Puglian olive groves. One of the most widely grown olive varieties is the Bella di Cerignola.

A fisherman prepares his nets for a day at sea. The city is renowned for mussels, lively fish markets and local restaurants.

Where Taranto differs radically from the rest of
the Salento is that its economy is not dependent
on agriculture, though a few places buck that trend.
The towns of Martina Franca, Cisternino and
Locorondo, for example, are surrounded by woodland
that is perfect for rearing pigs, so they produce a dry-
cured meat called *capocollo* or *coppa*. Its distinctive taste
comes from marinating the meat in *vino cotto* before
packing it into the animal's cleaned intestine and
leaving it to smoke over Macedonian oak, almond husks
and woody herbs. It is then cured for 100–180 days
before being sliced whisper thin and traditionally served
with fresh figs and a final drizzle of *vino cotto* to bring
out its dark, smoky flavour. Ideally, it might also come
with a chunk or two of bread from Laterza, which has
won plaudits for its flavour and aroma. The ancient
recipe combines semolina, water and yeast, and the
resulting dough is left to rise for six hours before being
baked on hot stones in furnaces fuelled by aromatic
olive or almond wood. The result is a satisfyingly
chewy loaf with an incredibly crispy crust. It can
support all manner of fillings, the local favourite
being *carne al fornello*, meat grilled over the same
aromatic woods.

In terms of fresh produce, the region has a long-
established association with clementines, and Palagiano
is the epicentre of their production – so much so that
it is known as the 'City of Clementines'. According
to local history, the fruit was introduced to the Gulf
of Taranto in the early eighteenth century by a monk
named Clement, who discovered it on a trip to Algeria.
This cross between a tangerine and an orange is almost
perfectly spherical and amazingly sweet, and did so well
in the local conditions that it has become the region's
predominant crop. La Clementina del Golfo di Taranto
earned itself IGP (*Indicazione Geografica Protetta*) status
in 2003.

ZUPPA DI NATALE

Christmas soup

Although, as the name makes clear, this soup is traditionally made at Christmas, it's a wonderfully satisfying dish that can be served whenever you like.

Preparation time: 25 minutes
Cooking time: 30 minutes
Serves 6

— 1 × 600 g / 1 lb 5 oz Altamura (semolina) bread, sliced
— 100 g / 3½ oz mild caciocavallo cheese, sliced
— 250 g / 9 oz turkey breast, boned
— 250 g / 9 oz mozzarella cheese, drained and sliced
— 1 litre / 1¾ pints (4¼ cups) meat stock
— 25 g / 1 oz (⅓ cup) grated Parmesan cheese, to serve
— salt and pepper

Preheat the oven to 180°C / 350°F / Gas Mark 4.

Arrange the bread on a baking sheet and toast in the oven, turning it as necessary so that both sides are lightly browned.

Layer half the toast in a 18 × 30-cm (9 × 12 inch) baking dish, followed by the caciocavallo and turkey. Season well. Top with the mozzarella and remaining bread. Pour half of the stock into the dish and bake, uncovered, for about 30 minutes, until golden brown on top and the turkey is cooked through.

Serve the rest of the hot stock in individual bowls. Each guest can then add their portion of pie and the desired amount of Parmesan.

MUSSELS

Cozze, as mussels are called in Italian, have been farmed in Taranto since ancient times, and the annual production rate along this stretch of coast is one of the highest in Italy. The mussel farms are sandwiched between two seas, the Mar Grande and Mar Piccolo, which form part of the Gulf of Taranto, and are among the largest in Europe. There are at least ten mussel farms looping off the Taranto shores, the largest of which is called the Ring of San Cataldo in honour of the regional capital's patron saint. While the mussel farms are an important source of food and income, they also employ over 1,000 specialist workers to harvest the crop and thus make a big contribution to the economic wellbeing of the city. The actual shellfish have an excellent flavour, unlike that of any other, a quality attributed to the *citri* – the freshwater springs that mix with the seawater to produce fat, yellow-fleshed mussels that are sweet and aromatic with no hint of bitterness. Local mussel specialties are many and varied, ranging from the simple fisherman's *Zuppa di mitili* ('Soldiers' soup') to raw mussels slurped like oysters with just a drizzle of lemon juice or vinegar. They may also come fried (*Cozze fritte*, see page 128), hot and crunchy, or stuffed *alla marinara*, tossed through pasta or risotto, or folded into a *tortiera*, an Italian omelette. There is only one thing aficionados insist on: that the mussels must be minutes-fresh from the shore.

The mussels are grown on ropes attached to the undersides of rafts in the water. They are then pulled to the surface when harvested.

Pages 130–1:
As the third largest city in southern Italy, Taranto sits right on the Ionian Sea coast.

COZZE FRITTE

Fried mussels

Recipes are endless when it comes to mussels. One of the most traditional ways of serving them is *arraganate* (sprinkled with chopped bread, garlic, parsley, oil and tomato), but they may also be boiled, then flavoured with oil and lemon, or used in the fragrant *zuppa alla marinara* (fish soup flavoured with tomato paste, onion and oil), or in a *tiella* (see page 106), a layered dish with rice and potatoes. This simple fried mussel dish makes a delicious start to a meal.

Preparation time: 40 minutes
Cooking time: 30 minutes
Serves 6

— 24–30 large mussels
— 2 eggs, beaten
— 100 g / 3½ oz (1 cup)
  dry breadcrumbs
— flour, for dusting
— vegetable oil, for frying
— salt

In a large saucepan with 2.5 cm / 1 inch boiling water, steam the mussels, covered, for 2 minutes. Then drain and rinse under cold water. Discard any mussels with broken shells or shells that do not open. Remove the mussels from the shells.

Place the eggs and breadcrumbs in separate shallow bowls. Sprinkle the mussels with flour, shaking off any excess. Dip them into the beaten egg and then into the breadcrumbs, making sure they are well coated.

Put enough oil in a deep saucepan to fill it one-third full. Heat to 190°C / 375°F or until a cube of bread browns in 20 seconds. Carefully add the mussels in batches and deep-fry for about 2 minutes or until the mussels are golden brown. Lift out with a slotted spoon and drain on paper towels. Season with salt and serve immediately.

TOMATOES

Few Italian regions have been quite so successful as Puglia in preserving a network of small- to medium-sized farms that are capable of producing excellent *pomodori* (tomatoes) in high yields. Fuelled both by local demand and a national and international customer base, Puglian producers have retained a strong link to their land, eschewing industrial methods of farming in favour of 'sticking to the way it's always been done' with extraordinary results.

La Motticella is the farm of local legend Paolo Petrilli, a veteran farmer-turned-winemaker, who's passionate about 'slow' agriculture. His neat, whitewashed estate outside Lucera is surrounded by honey-coloured wheat fields, razor-sharp lines of vines, and vast, bushy tomato plantations that yield many varieties, including the prized San Marzano.

The tomatoes are the firm's pride and joy, pruned according to the 'T' technique (borrowed from vine-growing), which concentrates the fragrance and flavour into the fruit. These top-notch tomatoes are later used in gourmet sauces and preserves so delectable that they have become known simply as 'luxury for the masses'.

A diverse assortment of tomatoes. The Puglian terrain and climate provides perfect conditions for a range of cultivars to prosper.

*Pasta and
tomato bake*

Preparation time: 30 minutes + 30 minutes for salting
Cooking time: 1 hour 10 minutes
Serves 10

— 2 kg / 4½ lb ripe tomatoes,
  halved
— olive oil, for brushing
  and drizzling
— 80 g / 3 oz (1¾ cups) fresh
  breadcrumbs
— ½ clove garlic, chopped
— 65 g / 2½ oz (¾ cup)
  pecorino cheese, grated
— 65 g / 2½ oz (¾ cup) Parmesan
  cheese, grated
— handful of parsley, chopped
— 500 g / 1 lb 2 oz broken
  rigatoni or ziti pasta
— salt and pepper

For the sauce:
— 100 ml / 3½ fl oz
  (scant ½ cup) olive oil
— 2 cloves garlic
— 800 g / 1¾ lb (3⅓ cups)
  canned chopped tomatoes
— salt and pepper

Score the uncut surface of the tomatoes in a crisscross
pattern and place them on a plate, cut side up. Sprinkle
with salt and leave to draw out their moisture for
30 minutes.

Meanwhile, make the sauce. Heat the oil in a frying pan
or skillet over medium heat and brown the garlic cloves.
Discard the garlic, then add the tomatoes. Season and
cook for about 10 minutes. Season.

Preheat the oven to 220°C / 425°F / Gas Mark 7.
Brush a large baking dish with oil.

Put the breadcrumbs in a bowl and mix in the chopped
garlic, pecorino, Parmesan and parsley.

Pat the tomatoes dry with paper towels. Arrange
half of them in the prepared dish and sprinkle with
half the breadcrumb mixture. Drizzle with oil and bake
for about 10 minutes, until the top is golden brown.
Set aside.

Cook the pasta in a large saucepan of boiling salted
water until al dente. Drain, then toss in the tomato
sauce and a little of the breadcrumb mixture. Spread
over the baked tomatoes. Arrange the remaining
tomatoes over the pasta. Sprinkle the surface with
the remaining breadcrumb mixture, drizzle with oil
and bake for 15 minutes, until golden brown on
top. Allow to stand for a few minutes before serving.

ALTAMURA BREAD

Loaves rising in renowned bakery Panificio e Biscottificio Fratelli di Gesù s.n.c. in Altamura. The bakery was established in 1838 and remains within the di Gesù family.

They say the simple things in life and gastronomy are the hardest to do, so this seemingly simple farm-house loaf, which was awarded PDO status in 2003 – the first bread in Europe to receive such an accolade – must be pretty close to perfect. The recipe dates back to the sixteenth century, when it was the pride and joy of communal bakeries in Altamura in the Murge district of Bari. Indeed, some of these bakeries are still used today by sticklers for tradition. Boasting an aroma that is said to drive people mad with longing, the bread also has an exceptional flavour as a result of the superb local ingredients it contains – namely, top-quality durum wheat and semolina, plus sweet local spring water. Its dense crust, which PDO regulations specify must be at least 3 mm/⅛ inch thick, protects the delicious dough within. In medieval times, banquets hosted by the bon vivant Federico II of Swabia at his court in Palermo always included large loaves of crusty bread, believed to be the forebears of the famous *pane di Altamura*. The Pugliese like it best as rustic *bruschette* drizzled with olive oil and sprinkled with tiny shreds of the equally revered *peperone di Senise* (dried chilli, see page 230) of Basilicata.

Pages 138–9:
DiGesù bakery's popular and aromatic tomato focaccia sizzling in the oven.

PASTA E CAVOLFIORE

Pasta and cauliflower

Don't be misled by the prosaic name of this recipe. True, it's a combination of simple ingredients, but this dish is extremely tasty. Top with fried breadcrumbs for extra texture, or offer grated cheese on the side.

Preparation time: 25 minutes
Cooking time: 30 minutes
Serves 6

— 1 large cauliflower (about 1 kg / 2¼ 1lb), broken into florets
— 500 g / 1 lb 2 oz broken capunti or ziti pasta
— 3 tablespoons olive oil, plus extra for drizzling
— 1 clove garlic
— 100 g / 3½ oz smoked pancetta cubes
— 10 cherry tomatoes, diced
— 1 dried chilli, crushed
— grated Parmesan cheese, to serve
— salt and pepper

Put the cauliflower into a large saucepan of boiling salted water and cook for 5 minutes, until tender. Drain and set aside, reserving the cooking water.

Cook the pasta in the boiling cauliflower water for 10 minutes, or until al dente.

Meanwhile, heat the oil in a frying pan or skillet, add the garlic and fry over medium heat until browned. Discard the garlic, then add the pancetta, tomatoes and chilli to the oil and fry for 5–6 minutes, until soft.

Drain the pasta, then add to the pan along with the cauliflower and seasoning. Drizzle with olive oil. Stir well, scatter with Parmesan and serve.

LEMONS

The *giardini di limoni* (lemon gardens) of Sorrento may bear the mark of the IGP on their vibrant skins, but the Pugliese would argue that the biggest, juiciest lemons come from the heel of Italy, where they grow in abundance. Originally from South-east Asia, the fruits were exchanged for gold in medieval times by canny Middle Eastern traders, and the trees fast became an important part of the Italian landscape, literally holding it together with their strong, deep roots. Bright-tasting citrus has since become an essential part of many regional specialities, including heavenly Limoncello, the local lemon-flavoured liqueur; jars of plump, tender artichokes infused with richly scented lemon oil; a moist olive oil and lemon cake that is the pride of Lecce; savoury gremolata made of chopped parsley and lemon zest that adds zip to grilled meat and fish; and the thirst-quenching lemon granita that refreshes the palate after the most extravagant of Pugliese feasts. Nowadays, gourmet travellers tour lemon groves as they would vineyards, as impressed as Italians were when they first embraced this most versatile of fruits as their own.

Lemons are plentiful in southern Italy and used extensively in the cuisine. Regional specialities include Limoncello, the popular lemon-flavoured liqueur, which is often served after dinner.

MELANZANE RIPIENE AL SUGO

Stuffed aubergines (eggplants) with tomato sauce

Preparation time: 30 minutes + 35 minutes standing
Cooking time: 30 minutes
Serves 6

— 6 long aubergines (eggplants)
— 1 tablespoon coarse salt
— 2 tablespoons olive oil, plus extra for deep-frying
— 2–3 tablespoons capers
— 3 eggs
— 70 g / 2¾ oz (¾ cup) Parmesan cheese, grated, plus extra for sprinkling
— 300 g / 10 oz (6½ cups) fresh breadcrumbs
— 400 ml / 14 fl oz (1¾ cups) tomato sauce
— salt and pepper

Halve the aubergines (eggplants) lengthways, then scoop out the flesh, reserving the empty shells. Place the flesh in a bowl, add the coarse salt and cover with water. Leave to stand for 30 minutes. Drain well, then use your hands to squeeze out any remaining water.

Preheat the oven to 180°C / 350°F / Gas Mark 4.

Heat 2 tablespoons of oil in a saucepan and fry the aubergine flesh for about 5 minutes, until soft and lightly browned. Drain on paper towels, then place in a bowl. Add the capers, eggs, cheese and breadcrumbs to form a soft stuffing. Season to taste. Fill the reserved aubergine shells with the stuffing.

Heat a 2.5-cm / 1-inch depth of oil in a frying pan or skillet until very hot. Put the filled shells in the pan, stuffing side down, and fry for about 3 minutes, until browned and heated through. Lift out with a slotted spoon and drain on paper towels.

Pour the tomato sauce into an oven dish, arrange the fried aubergines in it, stuffing side up, and bake for 20 minutes. Allow to stand for 5 minutes before serving. Sprinkle with grated Parmesan to serve.

AGNELLO ALLE ERBE
AROMATICHE

Lamb with aromatic herbs

Lamb is very popular in Puglia, perhaps partly because beef was traditionally very expensive. Although that's no longer the case, old habits die hard, and lamb is still the meat of choice for many people.

Preparation time: 30 minutes + 15 minutes maceration
Cooking time: 1 hour 25 minutes
Serves 6

— 100 ml / 3½ fl oz (scant ½ cup) red wine vinegar
— 2 tablespoons chopped rosemary, plus extra to garnish
— 2 tablespoons chopped sage leaves, plus extra to garnish
— 2 bay leaves
— 30 g / 1 oz (¼ cup) plain (all-purpose) flour
— 1.5 kg / 3¼ lb shoulder of lamb, cut into 4-cm / 1½-inch pieces
— 3–4 tablespoons olive oil
— 1 clove garlic
— 3 anchovy fillets, chopped
— 500 g / 1 lb 2 oz tomatoes, skinned, seeded and diced
— salt and pepper

Pour the vinegar into a bowl, add the herbs and leave to macerate for 15 minutes. Remove and discard the bay leaves.

Put the flour on a plate or in a plastic bag, add the lamb, season and toss to coat. Sift to remove any excess flour.

Heat the oil in a large frying pan or skillet, add the garlic clove and fry until browned. Discard the garlic, then add the anchovies and stir until they disintegrate. Add the lamb pieces and brown thoroughly on all sides. Pour the vinegar mixture over the meat and heat until evaporated. Season to taste.

Add the tomatoes to the lamb. Cover and cook for about 1 hour, until the meat is tender. Alternatively the casserole dish can be placed in an oven preheated to 150°C / 300°F / Gas Mark 2 and cooked for 1 hour. Taste and adjust the seasoning. Transfer to a warm serving dish and garnish with sprigs of fresh rosemary and sage.

PRIMITIVO DI MANDURIA

At the time of writing, there is talk of a wine renaissance in Puglia, particularly among growers dedicated to endemic grapes, such as Primitivo di Manduria. Although this grape is grown in the USA as Zinfandel, the Primitivo name is little known outside Italy, even though it produces arguably the greatest European red wine that almost nobody has heard of. The vines are grown in sixteen municipal areas between the provinces of Taranto and Brindisi, and since the wine has been awarded its own DOC – a badge of assured quality – it is gaining popularity. Unlike many other grapes grown for wine, the Primitivo variety is deliberately over-ripened before being picked, and this gives the wine its rich, voluptuous character of black-cherry ripeness with just a hint of herbs and spice. Like the land in which it is produced, it is brimming with personality. The best Primitivo di Manduria wines can be aged for up to ten years, and go superbly well with wintry game dishes and prime cuts of beef.

The Mediterranean climate provides the perfect conditions Negroamaro grapes, just one of the many varieties grown in the region.

BISCOTTI GLASSATI
ALLE NOCI

Iced walnut biscuits

Preparation time: 10 minutes
Cooking time: 50 minutes
Serves 18–24

— 250 g / 9 oz (2½ cups)
shelled walnuts
— 350 g / 12 oz (1¾ cups)
caster (superfine) sugar
— 2 egg whites
— pinch of salt
— 1 tablespoon freshly
squeezed orange juice

Preheat the oven to 120°C / 250°F. Line a baking sheet
with baking (parchment) paper.

Put the nuts in a blender or food processor with
100 g / 3½ oz (½ cup) of the sugar and whiz until finely
chopped. Transfer to a bowl. Add 1 egg white, a pinch
of salt and another 100 g / 3½ oz (½ cup) of the sugar
and stir until a smooth mixture forms.

Spread the mixture into a square about 5 mm / ¼ inch
thick on the prepared sheet, smoothing the edges with
a spatula.

Mix the remaining sugar, egg white and orange juice
in a bowl until a thin icing forms. Pour it over the
mixture. Using a knife dipped in cold water, cut the
dough into 4-cm / 1½-inch squares.

Bake for about 50 minutes, then cool on a wire rack
and serve.

V

BRINDISI

BRINDISI

With a population of just 90,000, Brindisi is a lively little town with a deep natural harbour shaped like a crab's pincer on the south-eastern tip of the peninsula. It was founded 3,000 years ago, conquered by everyone from the Byzantines and Normans to Vandals, Goths and Arabs, and somehow became one of the most convivial places in the country. Locals are noted for their love of eating, drinking and generally engaging with whoever happens to be passing. Perhaps more than anywhere else in the region, Brindisi has a deep attachment to the *passeggiata* (evening stroll). This allows people to keep an eye on each other while snacking on a wide variety of bread-based street food, including *panzerotto* (a deep-fried calzone) stuffed with molten mozzarella, focaccia anointed with the region's intensely fruity Collina di Brindisi olive oil, and *rustici* (rough) pastries stuffed with anything from tomatoes to spinach.

Brindisi's passionate love affair with food stems from its harbour being an important stop for seafaring traffic plying between such far-flung places as Constantinople (now Istanbul) and the East Indies (Caribbean). Invariably the ships were laden with unusual foodstuffs, such as cinnamon, nutmeg, tomatoes, chillies and potatoes. Both these and culinary ideas were enthusiastically embraced by the local populace. The sea, likewise, was a great provider, and fishermen still land their glittering catch straight onto the slippery cobblestones of the harbour. This is whisked away almost immediately by beady-eyed housewives and restaurant owners, who turn it into *ciambotto* – a delicately spiced Mediterranean stew, and *tiella* (see page 106), a rib-sticking peasant dish containing rice, potatoes and mussels.

The city limits blur into the lush, surrounding countryside, one of the most beautiful and fertile landscapes in all of Italy. Here are grown a wonderful

Page 152:
Ostuni, known as 'the White Town', sits on top of a hill and is renowned for its whitewashed walls.

The *frisa* is a bagel that has been baked whole, cut in half and then baked again. To serve, they are soaked in water, then topped with tomato, basil and olive oil.

Puglia produces 40 per cent of Italy's olive oil. Its land is host to millions of *ulivi secolari*, or ancient olive trees.

variety of vegetables, so it's little wonder that vegetarian antipasti feature so heavily in homes and restaurants. Local cooks produce a staggering array of salads and appetizers that recall the *mezze* of Lebanon and the multiple cooked salad courses of Morocco. These are always accompanied by large baskets of *taralli* (ring-like crackers, see page 260) flavoured with fennel seeds, or *pucchette*, a softer savoury biscuit studded with olives, which are used as scoops and add a satisfying crunch to treats such as courgettes (zucchini) stuffed with nutmeg-laced béchamel, sweet pumpkin mousse and oranges stewed in *vino cotto*.

Brindisi is said to make the best *vino cotto* by slowly cooking grape juice for several hours until it thickens and reduces. Known as *defrutum* in ancient Rome, it was used to preserve and sweeten foods, and modern cooks will drizzle it over grilled meats or poultry, or over mature hard cheeses and risotto to give a pleasing acidic kick. The vinegar-based version, *agrodolce*, is popular as a salad dressing or as a topping for ice cream.

This endlessly imaginative treatment of fruit and vegetables came about not so much by design as through necessity. Meat was expensive, so it was eaten with a certain ceremony and no part of it was wasted. Today, dishes such as *turcinieddi* (lamb kebabs made with offal [variety meats]) and *bombette* (thin slices of grilled beef and ham) are must-haves at local festivals, and any form of meal in the region is unthinkable without a glass of local wine to go with it. In fact, the Italian phrase for 'a toast' is *un brindisi*, and according to local lore King Herod himself demanded wines from Brindisi to stock his cellar.

Pages 158–9:
From the end of August to the beginning of September, grape harvesting occurs across the sun-blushed Pugliese landscape. Olives are picked in the cooler month of October.

The region's Arab legacy is perhaps best seen in what are now two quintessentially Italian products: coffee and almonds. These come together in *caffè ghiaccio con latte di mandorla* – iced espresso topped with almond milk. What could be more emblematic of the region's mixed heritage?

RICOTTA FORTE

The Pugliese have a knack for coaxing big, robust flavours out of seemingly simple ingredients such as the tangy cheese known as *ricotta forte* or *ricotta scanta* (both *forte* and *scanta* mean 'strong'), which verges on the genius.

Ricotta, meaning 'recooked', is made when whey is heated and forms a fine curd, which is then strained. At this point it becomes fresh ricotta, which is best eaten within a day or so, but if you allow the cheese to ferment, as the canny Pugliese do with careful stirring and salting every day or so, the curds gradually thicken and sour, and within a few months become the pungent, soft cheese that is packed into terracotta jars and used liberally across the region. They are truly the masters of getting the most out of each ingredient.

Goat's milk *ricotta forte*, from the hills near Brindisi, is particularly sought after. Spread on toast and topped with salted anchovies, it makes an excellent canapé to serve with crisp white wine.

Ricotta forte has a soft, smooth consistency but is very different from its more famous, mild and creamy cousin – ricotta.

GNOCCHI DI RICOTTA CON PESTO DI ZUCCHINI E TARTUFO

Ricotta gnocchi with courgette pesto and truffle

— 400 g / 14 oz (1¾ cups) drained goat's milk ricotta cheese
— freshly grated nutmeg
— 5 tomato skins
— 400 g / 14 oz (2⅓ cups) semolina
— black truffle flakes, to serve
— salt and pepper

For the pesto:
— 4 small courgettes (zucchini)
— 30 g / 1 oz (¼ cup) walnuts, shelled
— 5 ice cubes
— 1 tablespoon good-quality extra-virgin olive oil, plus extra for drizzling
— 1 small bunch basil, plus extra for garnishing
— salt

Preparation time: 30 minutes + 8 hours resting
Cooking time: 2 hours + 10 minutes
Serves 4

Cream the ricotta in a bowl. Add nutmeg and salt to taste, then spoon the mixture into a piping (pastry) bag fitted with a 1.5-cm / ½-inch plain nozzle. Pipe balls of the mixture onto a tray, cover and place in the refrigerator for about 8 hours.

Preheat the oven to 50°C / 120°F or lowest gas mark setting. Arrange the tomato skins in an ovenproof dish and place in the oven for about 2 hours.

To make the pesto, cut the courgettes (zucchini) in half lengthways and scoop out the pulp. Place it in a saucepan of boiling salted water and cook for 1½ minutes, until just soft. Drain, cool in iced water, then drain again. Place in a blender with the walnuts, ice cubes, olive oil, basil and salt and whiz until creamy. Transfer to a heatproof bowl and set aside.

Put the semolina on a large plate and roll the ricotta balls in it until well coated. Place in a saucepan of boiling salted water and cook over medium heat for 3–4 minutes. Drain well.

Place the bowl of courgette pesto over a saucepan of simmering water and heat through. Spoon it into the centre of 4 bowls. Place the gnocchi on top and garnish with flakes of black truffle, basil and tomato skin. Sprinkle with pepper and drizzle with oil before serving.

TORTA DI BIETOLINE
E RICOTTA

Chard, also known as Swiss chard, has green leaves, but the ribs and stalks come in several different colours. It doesn't matter what colour you opt for: the main thing is to use young and tender leaves.

Chard and ricotta pie

Preparation time: 20 minutes + 30 minutes soaking
Cooking time: 30 minutes
Serves 8

First make the pastry. Put the flour in a bowl and mix with the oil and 100 ml / 3½ fl oz (scant ½ cup) water. (No salt is needed.) Shape the dough into a fat cylinder, then cut into 4 equal pieces. Lightly flour a work counter and roll each piece of dough into a thin 20 × 25-cm (8 × 10-inch) sheet. Use 2 sheets to cover the bottom of the dish.

Preheat the oven to 190°C / 375°F / Gas Mark 5. Line the bottom and sides of a 20 × 25-cm (8 × 10-inch) baking dish with baking (parchment) paper.

Pour 475 ml / 16 fl oz (2 cups) salted water into a large saucepan, bring to a boil and add the chard. Cook for 2–3 minutes or until tender, turning the chard over frequently to ensure it cooks evenly. Drain and refresh under cold running water. When cool, squeeze the chard dry with your hands.

Place the chard a bowl and mix in the ricotta, Parmesan, onion, egg and seasoning. Spread the mixture in the pastry-lined dish and cover with the remaining sheets of pastry. Using a fine skewer, prick the pie several times almost down to the pastry base. Sprinkle the surface with the oil and 4 tablespoons water. Bake for about 30 minutes, until the pie is golden brown and piping hot. Leave to stand for 5 minutes before serving.

— 500 g / 1¼ lb Swiss chard leaves and tender stalks, soaked in salted water for 30 minutes
— 250 g / 9 oz (1 cup) ricotta cheese
— 80 g / 3 oz (1 cup) grated Parmesan cheese
— 1 small onion, chopped
— 1 egg, beaten
— 4 tablespoons olive oil
— salt and pepper

For the pastry:
— 500 g / 1 lb 2 oz (4 cups) plain (all-purpose) flour
— 6 tablespoons olive oil

OLIVES

Cerignola olives, the largest in the world, have a mild flavour and meaty texture, which many consider to be the finest available. The variety was probably introduced from Aragón in Spain around 1400, and became celebrated thanks to the development of the *sistema sivigliano* – a process that involves infusing the olives in a mixture of ash, quicklime and hot water to remove any bitterness. After that, they are rinsed and placed in a brine (salt solution) containing thyme and bay leaves. The majority are left a vivid green or black, but food colouring is added to some to create cherry-red olives.

Cerignola olives became so popular that by the early nineteenth century they were being shipped as far away as the United States in huge wooden barrels called *vascidd*, which could hold up to 1,000 kg/1 tonne. The olives were (and still are) grown organically on numerous small farms, then processed by a cooperative called *La Bella di Cerignola*. Although now a very large-scale operation, it uses the same artisanal techniques to produce its range of preserved olives, oils and tapenades. In fact, it received its own PDO status in 2000. Top of the line is the PDO Bella della Daunia olive, celebrated for its unblemished skin, plum-like proportions and silky texture of the flesh.

Not all varieties of olives grown in Puglia are suitable as table olives – some are best used purely for oil production.

LINGUINE ALLA SEPIA

Cuttlefish ink linguine

Preparation time: 30 minutes + 1 hour resting
+ —20 minutes drying
Cooking time: 5 minutes
Serves 4

For the pasta:
— 200 g / 7 oz (1⅔ cups) '00' flour
— 2 eggs, beaten
— 1–2 cuttlefish ink sacs
— olive oil
— salt

For the sauce:
— 150 g / 5 oz canned tuna in olive oil, flaked
— 3 tablespoons salted capers, rinsed and patted dry
— 3 tablespoons olive oil

To make the pasta, place the flour in a mound on a work counter, make a well in the centre and add the eggs, ink and salt. Mix with your hands until a dough forms, then knead until soft and smooth. Flatten the dough into a disc. Coat with a little olive oil, then wrap in clingfilm (plastic wrap). Leave to rest at room temperature for 1 hour.

Roll the dough out on a floured surface into a rectangle about 3 mm / ⅛ inch thick. Flour the surface of the dough well, then loosely fold over 4 times from the short end of the rectangle. Cut into strips 5 mm / ¼ inch wide. Open out, shake off the excess flour and hang over the back of a chair covered by a towel to dry until the pasta is no longer tacky to the touch.

Put the tuna in a bowl with the capers and oil and stir together.

Bring a large saucepan of boiling salted water to a boil, add the linguine and cook for about 2 minutes or until al dente. Drain well, then mix with the tuna. Serve.

FENNEL

If there were a taste that somehow gathered the essence of Puglia into one mouthful, it would perhaps be the sweet, slightly aniseed flavour of *finocchio* (fennel). The best grows wild in the hills of Daunia in Foggia, where the seeds are used in sweet and savoury breads and pastries, and the delicate green fronds are scattered as an aromatic finish over salads. The cultivated bulb, turned white, juicy and swollen by piling earth up around the stalks, is used as a vegetable in its own right. It may be eaten raw, thinly sliced and dressed simply with oil and vinegar, or braised slowly in butter, sprinkled with shaved Parmesan and served as a side dish, or piled up beneath a roast shoulder of lamb, or preserved in olive oil and served with cod. In Greek mythology fennel was considered sacred, its woody stalk the bearer of fire, so it carried huge weight in symbolic culinary use. Since those times, its popularity has waned and grown again, and it's curious to think that during the nineteenth century fennel was eaten only by Jews.

Delicately flavoured, raw fennel provides a sweet, delicious crunch to traditional southern Italian dishes.

FINOCCHIETTI STUFATI

Braised wild fennel

Wild fennel, a very popular vegetable in Italy, can be found throughout region of Puglia. In this simple recipe it is boiled, then sautéed with oil and garlic, and finally flavoured with anchovies.

Preparation time: 20 minutes
Cooking time: 45 minutes
Serves 4

— 2 tablespoons olive oil
— 1 clove garlic, chopped
— 2 anchovy fillets, chopped
— 1 mild red chilli, sliced
— 500 g / 1 lb 2 oz wild fennel, chopped
— salt and pepper

Heat the oil in a saucepan over a medium heat, add the garlic, anchovies and chilli and sauté for 3–4 minutes until fragrant. Add the wild fennel, season, cover and cook over a low heat for about 40 minutes, or until the fennel is tender.

Serve the fennel hot, as a side dish with roast meat.

LEGUMES

'*I legumi sono la carne dei poveri*' – pulses (legumes) are the meat of the poor – goes a local saying, and it is indeed difficult to think of a more valuable crop than beans to one of the poorest regions in Italy. Not only do they provide highly nutritious and satisfying food, they also enrich the land by imparting nitrogen-fixing bacteria through their root nodules.

Farmers in southern Mediterranean countries, where beans grow well, have long known this, and conditions in Basilicata are perfect for growing many varieties, ranging from plump cannellini (navy) and borlotti (cranberry) beans to tiny Gargano beans, which are revered for their earthy taste and velvety texture. Among the best are Sarconi beans, grown in a vast area of the Agri Valley between Tramutola, Marsico Nuovo and San Martino d'Agri, and which were given their own IGP in 1996. They have been cultivated here for centuries thanks to the unique irrigation systems, the low summer temperatures and the high altitude (at least 6,000 metres/ 20,000 feet above sea level), which gives them more time to turn their sugars into starch, resulting in a sweeter flavour and a silkier texture.

Summer is the optimal time to tuck into beans with such enticing names as rampicanti, verdolini, napolitanu avuti, tabacchino, maruchedda and San Michele, and in the middle of August each year, restaurants across the valley showcase the very best traditional recipes, including a hearty soup, beans with early porcini mushrooms, and flat sheets of *lagane e fagioli* (lagane pasta and beans).

In mid-August, Puglian restaurants celebrate the humble bean with a variety of local recipes.

Pages 175–6:
Puglia is home to many inviting ports, which provide the region with key trade, tourist and fishing spots.

FICHI AL CIOCCOLATO

Chocolate figs

More than fifty varieties of fig are grown in the Salento area and there are numerous ways of using them. In this recipe they are stuffed with almonds and baked with cocoa powder and wine. Another version suggests inserting a strip of candied orange peel into each fig and holding this 'stalk' while dipping them in melted chocolate. They are then left to dry before being placed in paper cases.

Preparation time: 30 minutes + 12 hours infusing
Cooking time: 15 minutes
Makes 18

— 500 g / 1 lb 2 oz dried figs
— 50 g / 2 oz (½ cup) roasted almonds
— 40 g / 1½ oz (½ cup) unsweetened cocoa powder
— vino cotto, for drizzling

Preheat the oven to 160°C / 325°F / Gas Mark 3.
Line a baking sheet with baking (parchment) paper.

Open up each fig, insert 1–2 roasted almonds and sprinkle with cocoa powder before pressing them closed.

Place the figs on the prepared sheet and bake for about 15 minutes, until softened.

Arrange the figs in layers in a bowl, sprinkling each layer with cocoa powder and drizzling with the vino cotto. Cover the bowl with clingfilm (plastic wrap) and set aside to infuse for 12 hours.

SFOGLIATELLE DI NATALE

Preparation time: 50 minutes + 10 hours standing +
overnight
Cooking time: 15 minutes
Serves: 8–10

Christmas pastries

The day before you want to make the pastries, put
the almonds in a bowl with the cocoa powder,
cinnamon, clove and sugar. Stir well, then cover with
clingfilm (plastic wrap) and set aside until needed.

The next day, put the raisins in a small bowl of warm
water and set aside.

To make the pastry, place the flour on a work counter,
make a well in the centre and add the eggs, sugar, oil
and wine. Mix with your hands to create a soft, smooth
dough, adding more wine if necessary.

Place the pastry on a lightly floured work counter and
roll into a large rectangle about 35 × 30 cm / 14 × 12
inches. Cut the pastry in half lengthways, then cut
crossways to make 8 rectangles about 15 cm / 6 inches
wide. Separate the rectangles and brush the upper
surface of each one with oil.

Drain the raisins, then stir into the nut mixture. Spread
a little jam (jelly) in the centre of each rectangle, then
add some nut mixture on top. Close the pastries by
folding one long edge over the other, then roll up
loosely from the short end to form pinwheels. Cover
with a cloth and let stand for 10 hours.

Preheat the oven to 180°C / 350°F / Gas Mark 4. Line
a shallow baking pan with baking (parchment) paper.
Arrange the pastries in the prepared pan, spacing them
about 1 cm / ½ inch apart. Delicately scatter or brush
a little water over them, sprinkle with sugar and
cinnamon, then bake for about 15 minutes, until dried
out but not brown. Serve warm or cold.

— 500 g / 1 lb 2 oz (5 cups)
  roasted and chopped
  unpeeled almonds
— 1½ tablespoons unsweetened
  cocoa powder
— pinch of ground cinnamon,
  plus extra for sprinkling
— 1 clove
— 1–2 tablespoons sugar,
  plus extra for sprinkling
— 2 tablespoons raisins
— vegetable oil, for brushing
— grape jam (jelly), for filling

For the pastry:
— 1 kg / 2¼ lb (8 cups) plain
  (all-purpose) flour, plus extra
  for dusting
— 2 eggs
— 100 g / 3½ oz (½ cup) caster
  (superfine) sugar
— 100 ml / 3½ fl oz (scant ½ cup)
  vegetable oil
— 3–4 tablespoons dry white
  wine, slightly warmed

VI

LECCE

LECCE

Situated as far south into the heel of Italy as you can go, Lecce is a largely flat region. It has just a few scattered hills no more than 200 metres/600 feet high, and is neatly enclosed within a rim of limestone cliffs carved into arches by the meeting of the Adriatic and the Ionian seas. The ancient Griko dialect, from when the area was part of Salentinian Greece, is still spoken in smaller towns and villages, giving the place a distinctive character quite unlike any other part of the peninsula.

The city of Lecce was founded over 2,000 years ago when Emperor Hadrian spent considerable time and resources fortifying the place, as well as adding lavish enhancements, such as a 25,000-seat amphitheatre. However, it is the astonishing Baroque churches and palazzi built in the seventeenth century by Spanish colonists that put Lecce on the map of present-day travellers and earned it the nickname 'Venice of the south'. No important monument has been left untouched by the Baroque: every limestone façade, including those of the Basilica di Santa Croce and the Palazzo dei Celestini, has ornate carvings of dragons, gargoyles and cherubs interlaced with playful floral motifs. It truly is a feast for the eyes.

Page 184:
A square in the city of Lecce, named after the political and historical figure Sigismondo Castromediano.

The church of San Giovanni Battista, or St. John the Baptist, was built in the seventeenth century.

The regional cooking itself is a showcase for *la cucina povera*, literally 'poor cooking' or 'peasant food', but is actually so much better than the name implies. It is the polar opposite of *haute cuisine* but displays an inventiveness that many chefs would dearly love to emulate. Locals relish every aspect of *la cucina povera*, from tasty street food that also accompanies aperitifs, to long drawn-out feasts that often segue straight from lunch into dinner. One of the most popular dishes at these feasts is *Rustico di Lecce*, a decadently rich concoction of creamy béchamel layered with tomatoes and mozzarella and encased within two circles of lard-based puff pastry. Typical to the region – you don't see this type of *rustico* in northern Puglia at all – it gives a sense of how deeply provincial Lecce cuisine is. It should come as no surprise that small cooking schools and at-home teachers showcasing local food have flourished in the last few years.

The famed *Melanzanata di Sant'Oronzo* (Saint Oronzo aubergine [eggplant] bake, see page 209) is a rich dish named after the patron saint of Lecce who evangelized Salento. His feast day is celebrated with extravagant dishes that were prepared for the enjoyment of the entire city population and rarely affordable the rest of the year. Unlike the Sicilian dish of the same name, this one has become increasingly baroque, and now includes veal meatballs, hard-boiled eggs and ham, which are alternately layered between fried aubergines, tomato sauce and mozzarella and baked au gratin. It is often served with *turciniedde* – a frugal, yet complex concoction of lamb or goat's innards flavoured with pecorino, lard, lemon, parsley, *diavolicchio* ('little devil' chillies from neighbouring Basilicata), more cheese and various herbs, rolled into sausages, skewered and grilled over hot coals.

Local fishermen while away the hours unloading the day's catch or mending tangled nets.

Delicious chocolate, lemon and fruit tarts on display at a local bakery. The Pugliese love their desserts.

Lecce's rib-sticking feasts are typically followed with sweets such as *pasticciotto*, a lemon custard pastry, and the inspired *spumoni*, an ultra-hard ice cream topped with a shot of hot coffee. Chocolate can also be served as a finale, especially that produced by Maglio Arte Dolciaria, a firm that has been processing cocoa beans and making chocolate in the region since 1875. The brand is held in great esteem for its loyalty to artisanal techniques, rediscovered traditional recipes and its own creativity. These include combining the chocolate with other ingredients from Salento, such as figs, almonds, walnuts and fruit, and producing an enticing range of fruit jams and jellies.

BROAD (FAVA) BEANS

Native to Puglia, broad (fava) beans have been grown there for thousands of years and form the basis of many hearty regional dishes. In some provinces they are used almost daily – fresh, dried, raw or cooked – in soups and salads, or made into a pureé, in which they are pounded together with wild chicory to a hummus-like consistency (see page 65).

Despite their long history, the beans' popularity took a long time to establish itself. In ancient Rome, people were wary of the black-spotted pods that yielded flat, glossy beans, and ate them only on days reserved for remembering the dead in case the departed cursed the living. Fast-forward a few centuries, however, and their status had risen considerably, thanks in no small part to Italy's sovereign Federico II, who had a taste for unusual foods. One of the most celebrated dishes of his court was *Pure di fave alla maniera di Federico II* (Broad [fava bean] mash in the style of Federick II, see page 192), in which honey gives it a distinctive sweet-and-sour character that has become typical of the region. According to a popular saying, this is *il sapore della giustizia* (the taste of justice), a reference to the right of all people, no matter how poor, to eat well.

Broad (fava) beans are an essential part of the Puglian diet and feature in many recipes.

PURE DI FAVE ALLA MANIERA DI FEDERICO II

Broad (fava) bean mash in the style of Frederick II

Inspired by Anna Martellotti's essay 'The Recipes of Federico II', this typical Puglian dish bears witness to the eccentric personality of the sovereign. Our version has been reworked with a sweet-and-sour sauce.

Preparation time: 10 minutes
Cooking time: 2 hours 30 minutes
Serves 4

— 350 g / 12 oz (2¼ cups) dried broad (fava) beans
— 1 sprig parsley
— 3 tablespoons vegetable oil
— 2 onions, chopped
— 2 tablespoons pale honey

Bring a saucepan of water to a boil over a medium-high heat and blanch the beans for about 20 minutes. Drain and rinse under running water, then transfer to a flameproof dish. Cover with water, add the parsley, bring to a boil and then reduce the heat and simmmer for 2 hours, without stirring (to prevent the beans breaking up). Shake the pan from time to time. Mash the beans vigorously to produce a thick purée. Divide among 4 dishes.

Heat the oil in a frying pan or skillet over medium heat, add the onions and cook for 8 minutes, or until translucent. Add the honey and cook for another few minutes, stirring constantly. Divide the bean purée among 4 dishes and spoon over the sauce. Serve immediately.

STRASCINATI

Strascinati are elongated pasta shells that are rolled and then dragged across a board to create ridges. Hailing from Potenza their origins date back to the sixteenth century and similar variations like *strisciati* (which are flattened after rolling into twists and then dimpled rather than dragged to better hold the sauce) are found all over the region.

There's a solid sense of the importance of *strascinati* in the region. Like *orecchiette* (from neighbouring Bari) it was an essential means of survival for poor families being cheap to make and reliably filling. Until the mid-eighteenth century, when the first commercial pastas started to appear, they were always made at home and it is a skill that is still revered today.

Many pasta processes in Puglia involve dragging the dough across a wooden surface, which creates little grooves for sauce to cling to.

STRASCINATI CON POMODORO E BASILICO

Strascinati with tomato and basil

Preparation time: 25 minutes + 50 minutes resting
Cooking time: 15 minutes
Serves 4

For the pasta:
— 600 g / 1 lb 5 oz (3½ cups) fine semolina
— grated pecorino cheese, to serve
— salt

For the sauce:
— olive oil, for frying and drizzling
— 2 cloves garlic
— 800 g / 1¾ lb (3⅓ cups) canned chopped tomatoes
— large bunch basil
— sea salt and pepper

To make the pasta, make a mound of flour on a clean work counter. Form a well in the centre, then add a pinch of salt and enough lukewarm water (about 650 ml / 12 fl oz [1½ cups]) to form a smooth, dense dough and knead for 10 minutes, or until smooth and springy. Cover with clingfilm (plastic wrap) and leave to rest for 30 minutes.

Next, pinch off a chunk of dough and roll between the surface and the palm of your hand until you have a long thin rope about 1 cm / ½ inch in diameter. Cut this into 4-cm / 1½-inch lengths, long enough to fit 3 middle fingertips put together.

To shape the pasta, press into the pasta with three fingers to make a soft indentation. Leave to rest on a floured surface for 20 minutes while you make your sauce.

To make the sauce, heat some olive oil in a skillet or frying pan, add the garlic and cook until fragrant. Add the tomatoes, half the basil and season, then simmer for 10 minutes until the tomatoes have reduced.

Bring a saucepan of salted water to a boil, add the pasta and cook for 4–5 minutes or until they float to the top. Drain the pasta reserving a cupful of the pasta water. Tip the drained pasta into the sauce and mix well, add a little of the pasta water to loosen the sauce if needed and drizzle with oil. Scatter over the remaining basil leaves and finish with pecorino.

CICERI E TRIA

Preparation time: 50 minutes + 1 hour resting
Cooking time: 3½ hours + 12 hours soaking
Serves 12

Chickpeas and tria

Drain the chickpeas (garbanzo beans) and put into a saucepan. Cover with cold water and bring to a boil. Drain and transfer to a flameproof casserole dish. Add a whole onion, the carrot, garlic and celery, cover with water, bring to a boil, then reduce the heat and simmer for 2 hours. Drain, reserving the cooking water. Discard the onion and celery.

To prepare the tria, combine the flours in a bowl and add just enough lukewarm water to form a firm dough. Knead for 10 minutes, or until dough is smooth. Flatten into a disc, lightly oil and wrap in clingfilm (plastic wrap) and rest at room temperature for at least an hour. Place on a lightly floured work counter and roll into a long rectangle about 3 mm / ⅛ inch thick. Cut the dough into strips about 5 mm / ¼ inch wide and 6 cm / 2½ inches long.

Heat the oil in a deep-fryer to 180°C/350°F, or until a cube of bread browns in 30 seconds. Fry one-third of the dough strips until golden. Drain on paper towels and set aside. Cook the remaining strips in the reserved cooking water until al dente, then drain, reserving a cupful of the water.

Chop the remaining onion, then cook in a saucepan with a little water and a pinch of salt until the liquid has evaporated. Add 2 tablespoons oil and the chilli and fry until brown. Add the tomatoes and cook for 10 minutes, then stir in the chickpeas. Purée half of this mixture and return it to the pan. Season to taste, then add the boiled tria and heat through, adding a little chickpea water if the mixture seems too thick. Transfer to a large dish, drizzle with olive oil and serve with the fried tria and grated cheese.

— 500 g / 1 lb 2 oz (2½ cups)
 dried chickpeas (garbanzo
 beans), soaked in water
 for 12 hours
— 2 onions
— 1 carrot
— 1 clove garlic
— 1 celery stalk
— 2 tablespoons vegetable oil,
 plus extra for deep-frying
— 1 chilli, seeded and chopped
— 500 g / 1 lb 2 oz (2¾ cups)
 chopped tomatoes
— salt and pepper

For the tria:
— 150 g / 5 oz (1 cup)
 semolina flour
— 150 g / 5 oz (1¼ cups) '00'
 flour, plus extra for dusting

To serve:
— extra-virgin olive oil
— grated Parmesan cheese

ARTICHOKES

A member of the thistle family, globe artichokes
have a tendency to be loved or loathed by the people
who consume them, not least for the Herculean effort
it takes to penetrate their armour-like leaves to get
to their rich, buttery heart. Southern Italians most
definitely fall into the former category – they grow
almost 50 per cent of the world's *carciofi* (artichoke)
crop – and come early autumn you'll see fields
of this ravishing jewel (the unopened flower bud of
the thistle) standing to attention across the region.

It is thought they were originally cultivated from the
wild cardoon and first arrived in Sicily with Turkish or
Moorish invaders. They have flourished in the South
ever since, particularly in Brindisi where they are a
much anticipated winter treat, having earned IGP status
for their velvety texture and an unparalleled sweet
nuttiness that makes them particularly good eaten raw.

When cooked they form the basis of many splendid
dishes including a decadent artichoke Parmigiana,
frittata combined with mint, or stuffed with tomatoes,
capers, anchovies and chillies and then baked until
oozing and tender. The most celebrated of all these
being the *Sfoglio a cerchi* (Artichoke pie, see page 204) –
a crisp pastry filled with luscious artichoke béchamel.

Pages 200–1:
At Gallipoli port,
fishermen sell their fresh
catch on the street where
their boats are docked.

Artichokes are grown in
abundance in southern
Italy. Harvested in winter,
they can be stuffed,
marinated or baked.

SFOGLIO A CERCHI

Artichoke pie

Preparation time: 1 hour + 40 minutes chilling
Cooking time: 1 hour 20 minutes
Serves 6–8

— 60 g / 2 oz (4 tablespoons)
  butter
— 25 g / 1 oz (¼ cup) plain
  (all-purpose) flour
— 300 ml / ½ pint (1¼ cups) milk
— 1 × 400 g / 14 oz can artichoke
  hearts or bottoms, drained
  and thickly sliced
— 25 g / 1 oz (¼ cup) grated
  Parmesan
— salt and pepper

For the pastry:
— 375 g / 13 oz (3 cups) plain
  (all-purpose) flour, sifted,
  plus extra for dusting
— 100 g / 3½ oz (½ cup) lard,
  chilled and cut into 1-cm /
  ½-inch dice
— 2 eggs
— 1 teaspoon salt

To make the pastry, put the flour into a bowl. Reserve
1 tablespoon of the lard and set aside. Add the
remaining lard to the bowl, along with 1 egg and the
salt and mix together, adding just enough water to form
a smooth, medium-soft dough. Wrap with clingfilm
(plastic wrap) and chill for 30 minutes.

Melt 40 g / 1½ oz (3 tablespoons) of butter in a
saucepan. Add the flour and stir constantly until smooth
and hazelnut in colour. Pour the milk in slowly, stirring
briskly, and bring to a boil. Immediately reduce the heat
and simmer for 10 minutes, stirring occasionally.

Put the remaining butter into a frying pan or skillet,
add the artichokes and fry for 15 minutes. Season,
then stir the artichokes and Parmesan into the sauce.

Place a little less than half of the pastry on a lightly
floured work counter and roll out to form a very thin
round 25 cm / 10 inches in diameter. Place on a baking
sheet. Melt the remaining lard and brush it over the
pastry. Chill for 10 minutes.

Preheat the oven to 200°C / 400°F / Gas Mark 6.

On a baking sheet lined with baking (parchment)
paper, roll the remaining pastry into a 28-cm / 11-inch
round. Spoon the filling into the centre of the pastry,
leaving a border of 2.5 cm / 1 inch. Beat the remaining
egg and use it to brush the edges of the pastry. Carefully
place the top pastry layer over the filling and crimp the
edges. Brush the top with beaten egg and bake for
40–45 minutes or until golden brown. Serve warm or
at room temperature.

SEMOLINA

The principal ingredient of pasta is durum wheat, which is ground into fine semolina, then mixed with eggs and water. Among the best producers in the south are the Cavalieri family, who have grown wheat since the early 1800s. When hit by the agricultural crisis that followed the unification of Italy in 1872, they had to rethink their livelihood, and this led to them constructing their first millstones for grinding the wheat into semolina. By 1918 they had founded the Antico Pastificio Benedetto Cavalieri in Maglie, Lecce, with the aim of producing the highest-quality dried pasta in the country.

The company remains devoted to the old way of doing things, and the recipe has never changed, using exactly the same mix of semolina types, selected from exactly the same land as the family were farming nearly 100 years ago, and using exactly the same traditional techniques: prolonged mixing of the dough, slow kneading to maximize elasticity, lengthy pressing to remove moisture and finally slow drying.

It was in the last part of the process that the Cavalieris began to innovate. Traditionally, pasta had always been hung out to dry in the streets, but they adopted the new *metodo Cirillo*, which involved building special rooms that allowed the temperature to be controlled by means of hot water heaters and fans. The family now makes 32 different kinds of semolina pasta, as well as eight different kinds of wholewheat pasta, every packet signed off with the family name as an assurance of its heritage and quality.

Built in the eighteenth century, the church of Alcantarine has an iron cross and statues of St Anthony of Padua and Raphael the Archangel.

MELANZANATA DI SANT'ORONZO

Saint Oronzo aubergine (eggplant) bake

Preparation time: 1 hour
Cooking time: 1 hour 25 minutes
Serves 8

Put the flour and beaten eggs in 2 separate shallow dishes. Heat a one-third depth of oil in a deep frying pan or skillet. Dip the aubergine (eggplant) slices in the flour and then the beaten egg and fry a few at a time until crisp and brown. Carefully lift out with a slotted spoon or tongs and drain on paper towels. Season generously with salt.

To make the meatballs, pour the milk into a shallow bowl and soak the bread slices in it. Put the veal in a separate bowl with the Parmesan, pecorino, eggs, wine, garlic, parsley and seasoning. Squeeze the bread dry and add just enough to the meat mixture to give a moist consistency.

Take spoonfuls of the meat mixture and roll into balls. Add enough oil to a frying pan to coat the base, then fry the meatballs in batches until browned.

Preheat the oven to 200°C / 400°F / Gas Mark 6.

Spread a few tablespoons of the tomato sauce over the base of a baking dish. Arrange a layer of aubergine on top, sprinkle with some prosciutto and mozzarella, a few meatballs, a few slices of hard-boiled egg and more spoonfuls of tomato sauce. Continue making layers like this, finishing with a layer of aubergine coated with the sauce and sprinkled with the Parmesan. Bake for 25 minutes, or until the surface has browned. Leave to stand for 5 minutes before serving.

— plain (all-purpose) flour, for coating
— 2 eggs, beaten with a little salt
— vegetable oil, for frying
— 4 aubergines (eggplants), peeled and sliced lengthways
— 500 ml / 18 fl oz (2 cups) tomato sauce
— 150 g / 5 oz prosciutto, chopped
— 400 g / 14 oz mozzarella cheese, diced
— 3 hard-boiled eggs, sliced
— 150 g / 5 oz (1¾ cups) grated Parmesan cheese
— salt

For the meatballs:
— 100 ml / 3½ fl oz (scant ½ cup) milk
— 4 slices crustless bread
— 700 g / 1½ lb minced (ground) veal
— 50 g / 2 oz (½ cup) Parmesan cheese
— 50 g / 2 oz (½ cup) grated pecorino cheese
— 2 eggs, beaten
— 150 ml / 4 fl oz (½ cup) dry white wine
— 1 clove garlic, chopped
— 15 g / ½ oz (¼ cup) chopped parsley
— vegetable oil, for frying
— salt and pepper

PASTA DI MANDORLE CON FALDACCHIERA

Christmas cake with faldacchiera cream

Preparation time: 30 minutes
Cooking time: 20 minutes
Serves 8

— 1 kg / 2¼ lb (10 cups) very
   finely chopped almonds
— 500 g / 1¼ lb (2½ cups)
   granulated sugar
— 3 tablespoons unsweetened
   cocoa powder (optional)
— 2–3 tablespoons rum
   (optional)
— icing (confectioners') sugar,
   for rolling and dusting
— 34 slices sponge cake
— 100 ml / 3½ fl oz (scant ½ cup)
   brandy
— 4 tablespoons pear jam
   (preserves), ideally perata,
   made from petrusine pears
— coloured sugar-coated
   almonds, to decorate

For the faldacchiera cream:
— 2 egg yolks
— 1 tablespoon dry Marsala wine
— 2 tablespoons caster
   (superfine) sugar

First make the cream. Combine all the ingredients in a heatproof bowl set over a saucepan of simmering water (the bowl must not actually touch the water). Stir until the mixture thickens and coats the back of the spoon. Set aside to cool.

Put the almonds, sugar and cocoa powder (if using) into a bowl and add just enough water (flavoured with the rum if you like) to make a paste. Sprinkle a sheet of baking (parchment) paper with a spoonful of icing (confectioners') sugar and roll out the almond paste so it will be large enough to line the mould.

Dust the inside of your mould with icing sugar and place it, hollow side down, on the almond paste. Invert both mould and paste, using the paper to help you, then press the paste inside. Trim off the excess. Arrange the slices of sponge cake inside the lined mould, drizzle with the brandy, then spread with the pear jam (preserves). Spoon the *faldacchiera* cream over the top. Re-roll the remnants of almond paste and use to cover the cream.

To serve, invert the cake onto a plate and decorate as you like with the sugar-coated almonds. If covered with clingfilm (plastic wrap) and stored in the refrigerator, this cake will keep for up to a week.

VII

POTENZA

Bocconcini fritti di lampascioni 222
Fried hyacinth bulbs

Baccalà al forno con crema di lenticchie e peperoni 226
Baked salt cod with lentil cream and peppers

Rafanata 229
Potato cake

Spezzatino di Rionero 232
Rioneresi stew

Maiale ai pepperoncini sott'aceto 237
Pork with pickled peppers

Calzone di castagne 238
Chestnut pastries

Lagana chiapputa 240
Pasta and almond dessert

POTENZA

Perched above the Basento river valley in the Apennine Mountains, Potenza, in Basilicata, is one of the highest cities in Italy. It's a hodgepodge of architecture, thanks to innumerable uprisings and three major earthquakes that have nearly destroyed the place in the past, but the population has a predilection for rebellion and seems to endure even the toughest times. Perhaps this is helped by the mineral water that flows from the springs on Mount Vulture, an extinct volcano that dominates the landscape. The waters, sometimes flavoured with lemons or oranges, are said to have curative powers.

It is actually the towns around Potenza that are celebrated for their gastronomic riches. Moliterno, for example – the name means 'place where milk is produced' – grazes its animals among lush chestnut groves in the Val d'Agri, and their uniquely flavoured milk is used to make the town's world-renowned pecorino. Containing two-thirds sheep's milk to one-third goat's milk, the cheese ages perfectly here thanks to the cool mountain air that comes with being 750 metres / 2,500 feet above sea level. In the old days people from villages further down the mountain would take their 10-day old wheels of cheese up to Moliterno to age them for 90–150 days. Then, as now, the cheese would be rubbed with olive oil to prevent moisture loss, gradually darkening to a rich, golden hue and developing a flavour that is wonderfully nutty and sweet. In fact, the very best of them cost more than the greatest Parmigianos. Locally, pecorino is served with a hot red chilli jelly, made from the esteemed peppers of Senise (see page 231), accompanied by a glass of powerful Aglianico del Vulture red wine.

More chillies are eaten in Basilicata than anywhere else in Italy, the most common kinds being the *diavolicchi* (little devils) and *frangisello* (saddle breakers). Kitchens in the region always have a string or two hanging from the beams, ready to stir into the pot, be it a simple

Page 212:
A woman prepares artichokes, peeling and trimming them before soaking them in lemon-infused water.

A typical larder storing oil and all types of dried pasta famous to the region, from *orecchiette* to fusilli.

maccheroni di fuoco (long noodles with chilli, garlic and olive oil), *spezzatino* (pork stew with chillies, tomato, rosemary and garlic, see page 232), or the classic *ragù alla potentina*, served with *strascinati* (see page 194). The last dish is really more of a pot-roast, slices of meat being sprinkled with chilli, garlic, parsley, nutmeg and small pieces of pecorino, then rolled up in pancetta and slowly braised in a pan with olive oil, tomatoes and wine. As just these few examples demonstrate, oil (*olio*), garlic (*aglio*) and chilli (*peperoncino*) are the 'holy trinity' of ingredients in Basilicata, as ubiquitous as tomato ketchup in other parts of the world.

Another characteristic of Basilicata, and long before it became fashionable elsewhere, is nose-to-tail eating, in which no part of an animal goes to waste. For many generations it was simply crucial to survival, but even now, in more plentiful times, people continue the habit. It is encapsulated in the huge range of sausages and cured meats that people consume, but perhaps the most iconic dish is *pignata di pecora*. This lamb, mutton and sausage stew, containing tomatoes, chillies, onions and other vegetables, is scattered with pecorino cheese and cooked for several hours in an earthenware pot sealed with clay.

Such hearty eating often ends with a *digestivo*, a herbal liqueur that helps the digestion and is the perfect excuse to prolong lunch or dinner just a few minutes more. Among the best is the local Amaro Lucano produced by the Vena family in Pisticci, who have been making it to a secret recipe since 1894. The alcohol is infused with roots, herbs, spices and flowers that give it a bitter-sweet, chocolatey finish. It can be enjoyed neat, or over ice with a twist of orange and a dash of soda.

Pages 218–9:
As in Puglia, wine and olive oil are essential ingredients in Basilicatan cuisine.

LAMPASCIONI

Often inaccurately described as wild onions, *lampascioni* (also known as *lambascione, lampasciuolo, cipollaccio* and *lampone* in local dialects) are the bulbs of the tassel or grape hyacinth, and can often be found where cornfields and grapevines are abundant. Italians, who love to forage for food, regard *lampascioni* as a prized local delicacy, gathering them in late winter and early spring before the plant's purple flowers begin to appear.

The small bulbs were a precious treat among rural peasants as far back as the ancient Greeks, who believed they were a potent aphrodisiac with excellent diuretic and emollient properties. The philosopher Chrysippus extravagantly described them as 'ambrosia' when served on top of lentils. When cooked, the bulbs have a pleasingly bitter and pungent flavour that is much admired among Puglian gastronomes. They cannot be eaten raw, as a thick, bitter sap oozes from them when cut, but they pickle well.

Lampascioni can be used in many ways – to flavour oil, in antipasti, sautéed with other vegetables, sliced and cooked with tomato and eggs, beer-battered and fried (see page 222), roasted as a garnish for Broad (fava) bean and wild chicory purée (see page 65) and added to roast lamb.

Basilicatans love foraging for food, including *lampascioni*, mushrooms and black truffles.

BOCCONCINI FRITTI DI LAMPASCIONI

Fried hyacinth bulbs

Preparation time: 45 minutes
Cooking time: 30 minutes
Serves: 8–10

— 50 g / 2 oz (⅓ cup) plain (all-purpose) flour
— 2 eggs
— 2 tablespoons freshly grated pecorino cheese
— 1 teaspoon chopped parsley
— 1 clove garlic, chopped
— 125 ml / 4 fl oz (½ cup) iced beer
— 600 g / 1 lb 5 oz (3¾ cups) hyacinth bulbs or wild onions, quartered
— vegetable oil, for frying
— salt

Put the flour into a bowl and add the eggs, a pinch of salt, the cheese, parsley and garlic. Mix well, then stir in the beer to obtain a soft batter. While still stirring, add the onions.

Heat a 2.5-cm / 1-inch depth of oil in a frying pan or skillet until hot, or until a cube of bread browns in 30 seconds. Add a few spoonfuls of the batter and fry until golden brown and crispy all over. Drain on paper towels. Continue until all the batter has been used. Serve hot.

CACIOCAVALLO CHEESE

With its lush green pastures, Basilican farmers are able to rear excellent dairy herds, and consequently the area has a wide range of excellent dairy produce. Among them is caciocavallo cheese, a stretched-curd cheese made out of sheep's or cow's milk.

One type of caciocavallo comes from the rare Podolica cow, a breed which originated in the Ukraine. This particular breed grazes on the aromatic grasses of the region's lowlands, absorbing hints of bay, liquorice and fennel in the process. In June they are moved to high mountain pastures, where they nibble on blueberries, rose hips, juniper and hawthorn, which add sweetness and complexity to their milk. The shepherds make the cheese themselves while still at high altitude, stretching the curds into distinctive teardrop shapes and hanging them from wooden rods to mature. When they come down again in November, the shepherds bring the cheeses too, which they continue to mature for a year or more – up to twelve years in the case of the very best ones.

The result of the hanging time is an intensely complex cheese, with nutty and herbal flavours plus a subtle hint of smokiness, derived from the fires that kept the shepherds warm at night. Because of its superb quality, it is nicknamed the 'Parmigiano Reggiano of the south'.

A cheese stall with caciocavallo hanging from hooks. As the cheese ages it becomes darker in colour and develops a thick rind.

BACCALÀ AL FORNO CON CREMA DI LENTICCHIE E PEPERONI

Salt cod with lentil cream and peppers

Preparation time: 20 minutes + 4 days soaking
Cooking time: 50 minutes
Serves 4

— 300 g / 11 oz (1½ cups) lentils
— 2 cloves garlic
— 6 tablespoons extra-virgin olive oil
— 600 g / 1 lb 5 oz salt cod, soaked for 4 days in several changes of cold water
— 1 handful parsley, chopped
— 3–4 oregano sprigs
— 25 g / 1 oz (½ cup) fresh crustless breadcrumbs
— 100 g / 3½ oz (½ cup) small vine tomatoes, quartered
— 4 dried sweet peppers, thinly sliced
— salt

Put the lentils into a saucepan with 1 garlic clove and 2 tablespoons of the oil, cover with water and bring to a boil. Reduce to a simmer and cook gently for 20 minutes, until soft. Transfer to a blender or food processor, add some salt and purée until smooth.

Preheat the oven to 200°C / 400°F / Gas Mark 6.

Cut the cod into 4 pieces and place in a baking dish. Sprinkle with the parsley, oregano and breadcrumbs. Place the tomatoes and remaining garlic clove on top and drizzle with 2 tablespoons of the oil. Bake for 20 minutes.

Heat the remaining 2 tablespoons oil in a heavy-based frying pan or skillet. When hot, fry the peppers over a high heat to make them crunchy.

To serve, pour a ladleful of the lentil mixture onto the serving plates. Place a slice of cod on top, spoon over the cooking juices and tomatoes and garnish with a few pieces of crunchy pepper.

RAFANATA

Potato cake

Once fresh horseradish root has been grated, it is important to use it straight away or the pungent aroma and peppery flavour will be lost. This delicious recipe can be served as an accompaniment to meat or vegetables, or offered as a nibble with drinks.

Preparation time: 15 minutes
Cooking time: 1 hour
Serves 6

Cook the potatoes in a saucepan of boiling salted water until soft. Drain and dry in the hot pan for a few minutes, then mash them. Transfer to a bowl and allow to cool to room temperature. Mix in the eggs, breadcrumbs, horseradish and salt.

Heat the oil in a frying pan or skillet, add the potato mixture and flatten with a fork. Cook over a medium heat for about 10–15 minutes, ensuring both sides are browned. Carefully transfer to a plate and serve hot.

— 400 g / 14 oz floury potatoes
— 4 eggs, beaten
— 200 g / 7 oz (4½ cups) fresh crustless breadcrumbs
— 200 g / 7 oz (2¾ cups) horseradish root, peeled and grated
— 2–3 tablespoons oil
— salt

PEPERONI DI SENISE

Peppers, particularly those from Senise, are a cornerstone of Basilicata's rustic cuisine, and in 1996 were granted their own IGP (protected geographical status), which narrowly defines the region from which they can be said to originate. When fresh, they are often sliced and added to sauces, stuffed with meat or local wheat berries, or grilled and preserved in oil. More typically, you will see the peppers hung on long ropes and left to dry in the sun, which further concentrates their flavour. At this stage they are called *peperoni secchi* (dried peppers) and are used to impart sweet, smoky notes to soups, potato dishes and frittatas.

They are known locally as 'poor man's saffron', but their primary use is, of course, as a seasoning and preservative for the region's celebrated pork sausages and hams. Some argue that the dried peppers are at their best when simply fried in olive oil to make *peperoni cruschi*, a brittle, salty, umami-like ingredient, that is tossed with pasta and breadcrumbs to make the region's signature dish of the same name. On their own, *peperoni cruschi* are Basilicata's most addictive bar snack, the perfect accompaniment to a glass of locally produced Aglianico wine.

Senise is an ancient town nestled within the Pollino National Park, the largest in the country, and next to the impressive Monte Cotugno Lake.

SPEZZATINO DI RIONERO

Rioneresi stew

The recipe takes its name from the northern Basilicata town of Rionero, which is towered over by the extinct Vulture volcano. The area is famous for its attractive scenery and the production of Aglianico wine.

Preparation time: 10 minutes + 1 hour standing
Cooking time: 2 hours and 15 minutes
Serves 6

— 1 kg / 2¼ lb lean pork leg
— 100 ml / 3½ fl oz (scant ½ cup) vegetable oil, for coating and frying
— 2 cloves garlic
— 1 tablespoon lard (optional)
— 250 ml / 9 fl oz (1 cup) white wine vinegar
— 3 onions, thinly sliced
— 1 red chilli, seeded and chopped
— salt and pepper

Rub the meat with 3 tablespoons of oil and 1 halved garlic clove. Leave the meat to stand for 1 hour, then cut into bite-sized cubes.

Heat 4 tablespoons oil and the lard, if using, in a flameproof casserole dish. Add the remaining garlic clove, fry until brown, then discard it. Add the meat and brown it thoroughly. Pour in just enough vinegar to cover it, then heat until evaporated.

Add the onions and chilli. Season the dish, lay a sheet of baking (parchment) paper over it, then cover tightly with the lid and gently simmer for about 2 more hours over a very low heat. Serve hot.

SAUSAGE

Lucanica – Basilicata's beloved coiled pork sausage – is believed to have originated in ancient Rome, but is a typical Potenza dish. It has an intense aroma that is largely thanks to the Basilicata pig, which roams freely, feasting on the green hill pastures that imbue its flesh with sweet, herby flavours. Spicy and hot (chilli being another flavour that defines Basilicata), it is the prime product obtained from the pigs, and in many ways the essence of Basilicata nose-to-tail cooking.

The actual slaughter of the pig retains an air of respectful ritual in rural Basilicata to this day. In times past, the first blow of the knife was always symbolically reserved for the head of the family, who then handed the knife to the pork butcher for processing the carcass. These days a certified butcher must do the job, but the rest of the slaughter continues much as it always did. The lean, finely textured meat of the legs and shoulders is turned into aromatic, slightly piquant hams, while lesser cuts are made into *soppressata* (a type of salami), *capocollo* (a dry-cured cut of neck and shoulder muscle) and *pezzenta* (a robust sausage made from chopped lung, liver and sinews, generously flavoured with pepper and garlic).

One of the many types of sausages produced in Basilicata, *capocollo* is available spiced or sweet.

MAIALE AI PEPERONCINI SOTT'ACETO

Pork with pickled peppers

Using a fatty cut of pork for this dish gives the most tender result. If concerned about the fat content, cook it in an earthenware dish, and therefore at a lower temperature, rather than in metal. This allows the meat to release all its fat, which can then be skimmed off before serving.

Preparation time: 10 minutes
Cooking time: 30 minutes
Serves 6–8

Heat the oil in a flameproof casserole dish. When hot, add the meat and fry for a few minutes over a medium heat, until browned all over. Add the peppers, drizzle with a little hot water and cook for 20–25 minutes, or until tender.

Taste the mixture, then season. Serve immediately

— 100 ml / 3½ fl oz (scant ½ cup) vegetable oil
— 1.2 kg / 2½ lb diced pork
— 200 g / 7 oz (¾ cup) pickled sweet peppers, seeded and thinly sliced
— salt and pepper

CALZONI DI CASTAGNE

Chestnut pastries

Preparation time: 30 minutes + 10 minutes chilling
Cooking time: 45 minutes
Makes about 48

— 400 g / 14 oz (3½ cups) plain
  (all-purpose) flour
— 120 g / 4½ oz (10 tablespoons)
  softened butter
— 300 g / 11 oz (1½ cups) caster
  (superfine) sugar
— 7 eggs
— 2 tablespoons sweet
  white wine
— vegetable oil, for deep-frying
— honey, for brushing

For the filling:
— 200 g / 7 oz (1 cup) dried
  chickpeas (garbanzo beans),
  soaked in water overnight
— 200 g / 7 oz vacuum-packed
  chestnuts
— 3 tablespoons unsweetened
  cocoa powder
— 60 g / 2 oz (¼ cup) caster
  (superfine) sugar, to taste
— aniseed oil, to taste

To make the filling, put the chickpeas (garbanzo beans) and chestnuts in separate saucepans, cover with water and bring to a boil. Reduce heat and simmer for about 45 minutes, or until softened. Drain, then puree in a blender or food processor with the cocoa, sugar and aniseed oil until a paste forms. Set aside.

Heap the flour in a mound on a work counter, make a well in the centre and add the butter, sugar, eggs and wine. Mix with one hand until a dough forms. Shape into a flat disc and chill for 10 minutes.

Roll the dough out into a rectangle about 1 mm / 1⁄16 inch thick, then cut out 8 equal 5-cm / 2-inch squares. Place a teaspoon of the filling in the centre of each square and fold the dough over to form triangles. Press the edges together with a fork.

Heat a 2.5-cm / 1-inch depth of oil in a frying pan or skillet over medium–high heat until it's hot enough to brown a cube of bread in 30 seconds. Carefully fry the pastries, a few at a time, until golden brown. Drain on paper towels.

Transfer the pastries to a plate and brush a little honey over them before serving.

LAGANA CHIAPPUTA

Pasta and almond dessert

This is a traditional dessert from Acerenza, a village listed as one of the most beautiful in Italy. It is cooked to celebrate the feast of St Lucy, on 13 December.

Preparation time: 30 minutes
Cooking time: 15 minutes
Serves 6

— 1 tablespoon olive oil
— 100 g / 3½ oz (1 cup) dried crustless breadcrumbs
— 100 g / 3½ oz (1 cup) walnuts, chopped
— 100 g / 3½ oz (1 cup) almonds, chopped
— scant 3 tablespoons vino cotto

For the pastry:
— 500 g / 1 lb 2 oz (4 cups) bread flour, plus extra for dusting
— salt

First make the pastry. Put the flour into a bowl, add a pinch of salt and mix in just enough lukewarm water, a spoonful at a time, to form a smooth, firm dough. Place on a lightly floured work surface and roll the dough into a rectangle about 3 mm / ⅛ inch thick. Using a sharp knife, cut the dough into strips about 7.5 cm / 3 inches wide.

Lightly salt a large saucepan of boiling water and cook the *lagana* strips until al dente.

Meanwhile, heat the oil in a frying pan or skillet, add the breadcrumbs and fry over a medium heat until golden brown. Stir in all the nuts, then set aside.

Drain the *lagana* strips and arrange in layers on a serving plate, sprinkling each layer with the bread mixture and drizzling with the vino cotto. Serve straight away.

VIII

MATERA

MATERA

Page 242:
Lively markets and the
region's best eating exist
against the backdrop of
ancient buildings in
Matera.

A World Heritage Site since 1993, Matera is famous
for its ancient limestone cave dwellings, known as
sassi, which date from the Palaeolithic period and are
thought to be Italy's first human dwellings. Remarkably,
they were inhabited continuously until the mid-
twentieth century, and inspired Carlo Levi's book
Christ Stopped at Eboli, a damning account of the
poverty he witnessed here in the 1930s. The region
is also remarkable for having hundreds of rupestrian
churches carved out of the soft, volcanic hills. Some of
these date back to the earliest days of Christianity, and
were used and maintained until the 1950s. The whole
area underwent massive regeneration in the 1980s, and
there are now flourishing bars, restaurants and small
hotels, that offer some of the best eating in the region.

The local market in Matera is found on the via Ascanio
Persio, and local farmers flock down from the mountains
six days a week, bearing fruit and vegetables, foraged
herbs and weeds, meats, cheeses and bread. The local
cooking is as dramatic and unusual as the environs.
In the 1900s, during the Italian Colonial Wars that led
to the conquest of Ethiopia, Somalia and Eritrea, the
poverty-stricken inhabitants of Matera moved to Africa
in search of work. When they were called back during
the Second World War, they brought with them the
rare and unusual seeds of the red aubergine (eggplant),
which became particularly associated with the town
of Rotonda. In fact, it's not related to the aubergine at
all, but it is texturally similar and described in the Slow
Food Foundation's 'Ark of Taste' as a little spicy, a little
bitter and a little like a prickly pear. Unlike the more
common purple aubergine, it tends to be preserved
in oil or vinegar rather than used for cooking, and
is highly regarded.

The old part of town
consists of a maze of streets,
some of which lie on top
of the roofs of houses.

Piquant foods are generally popular in the Matera
region, and the *peperoni* (bell peppers) from Senise (see
page 231) are also much appreciated. They are hung

up to dry from every gable, resembling nothing so much as fairy lights, then are deep-fried in olive oil to make *peperoni cruschi,* a bar snack that comes out particularly around Christmas time, when friends and neighbours go from house to house to taste the new wine.

Like so many places in the region, Matera produces excellent bread – some say the best in Italy. The huge loaves are made entirely from bran and baked in oak-burning stone ovens. The huge size of the bread helps it to retain its aroma and freshness for longer than the average loaf. At one time every housewife made her own loaves, marking them with a family symbol or initials so they would be recognizable among all the others baked in the large communal ovens. There are still some community ovens to be found in the warren of streets in the old town, where local pastries are also taken for baking. Most important are the twice-baked *frisa,* which are rock hard, but keep indefinitely. They make fantastic bruschette if dipped in water to soften slightly, then topped with chopped tomatoes, olive oil, hot pepper paste and fresh basil. At the sweeter end of the spectrum are *strazzate,* flavoured with chocolate, almonds and *strega,* a local herbal liqueur, while *schiumette* are Matera's equivalent of *îles flottantes* (floating islands), made of egg whites, vanilla and orange zest, and served with Rosolio, a sweet rose-petal liqueur.

Blurring the lines between tradition and modernity is an enduring characteristic of Matera and its people. It might seem an unlikely place for the best ice cream outside of Rome, but many believe it to be so, especially when its makers come up with amazing flavours, such as tangerine and basil, lavender and blueberry, and salted liquorice.

An intricately decorated door to a house in one of the town's caves.

Pages 248–9:
The thirteenth century cathedral's bell tower watches over the city and forms the highest point in Matera.

TORTA SALATA DI PASQUA

This traditional Easter pie is common not only
in Basilicata, but also in Puglia, where it is known
by the name of *cuzzola*.

Easter savoury pie

Preparation time: 40 minutes + 1 hour chilling
Cooking time: 30 minutes
Serves 6–8

To make the pastry, place the flour in a mound on
a work counter, make a well in the centre and add
a pinch of salt and the lard. Rub together with your
hands until the mixture resembles breadcrumbs.
Mix the egg yolk with 4 tablespoons of cold water,
then add to the flour. Bring together to a dough with
your fingers, adding more water if required. Flatten
into a disc, wrap in clingfilm (plastic wrap) and place
in the refrigerator for 1 hour.

Preheat the oven to 200°C / 400°F / Gas Mark 6.

Cut off about two-thirds of the dough and roll out
on a lightly floured work counter into a disc about
3 mm / ⅛ inch thick. Use to line a shallow 24-cm /
9-inch tart pan.

Put the eggs in a bowl, add the pecorino and a pinch
of pepper and beat together. Stir in the salami.

Arrange the cheese slices inside the pastry case,
then pour the egg mixture over them.

Roll out the remaining dough and use to cover the
filling. Trim off the excess, then press the edges
together to seal. Beat the extra egg yolk and brush it
over the pastry lid. Bake for about 30 minutes, until the
pastry is golden brown. Allow to cool before serving.

— 3 eggs plus 1 yolk
— 2 tablespoons grated
   pecorino cheese
— 150 g / 5 oz salami, chopped
— 300 g / 11 oz fresh toma di
   pecorino cheese, sliced
— pepper

For the pastry:
— 300 g / 11 oz (2⅓ cups) plain
   (all-purpose) flour, plus extra
   for dusting
— 100 g / 3½ oz (½ cup) lard
— 1 egg yolk
— pinch of salt

FUSILLI CON LA MOLLICA

A good first course, this dish is tasty and slightly spicy.
The anchovies are not at all 'fishy' – they simply impart
a wonderful depth of flavour.

Fusilli with bread

Preparation time: 10 minutes
Cooking time: 25 minutes
Serves 4

Heat the oil in a frying pan or skillet. When hot, add
a pinch of chilli powder, the croutons and anchovies,
stirring until the anchovies have melted. Set aside.

Cook the fusilli in a large saucepan of salted boiling –
water until al dente. Drain and tip into the anchovy
mixture. Add the pecorino, then sauté the pasta over
a medium heat for a few minutes. Sprinkle with the
parsley and serve immediately.

— 2 tablespoons vegetable oil
— pinch of red chilli powder
— 100 g / 3½ oz (1 cup)
  crustless croutons
— 4 salted anchovies
— 350 g / 12 oz fusilli pasta
— 65 g / 2½ oz (¾ cup) grated
  pecorino cheese
— 2 tablespoons
  chopped parsley

LAGANE E CECI

Here is a typical dish for 19th March, the feast of
St Joseph. Also known as *piatto del brigante* (brigands'
dish), after the nineteenth-century robbers who loved
to eat it, this unusual dish can be found in Calabria
as well as Basilicata.

Preparation time: 30 minutes + 12 hours soaking
Cooking time: 2 hours 30 minutes
Serves 4

To make the lagane, mix the semolina with just
enough lukewarm water to form a dough. Knead the
dough for about 10 minutes, until smooth, then oil the
dough lightly and wrap in clingfilm (plastic wrap). Rest
for at least 1 hour before rolling out on a lightly floured
surface or passing through a pasta machine until 2 mm /
$\frac{1}{16}$ inch thick. Cut into strips about 2.5 cm / 1 inch wide.
Set aside.

Drain the chickpeas (garbanzo beans), then place in
a saucepan of fresh water with the bay leaf and boil,
covered, for 2 hours. Drain well and discard the
bay leaf.

Heat 2–3 tablespoons of oil in a frying pan or skillet.
When hot, brown the garlic clove, then discard it.
Add the tomatoes, a pinch of chilli powder plus
salt and pepper and cook over a medium heat for
5 minutes. Add the chickpeas and heat for 10 minutes.

Cook the lagane pasta in a large saucepan of boiling
salted water until al dente. Drain, then add to the pan
of sauce and leave to infuse for 5 minutes. Taste and
adjust the seasoning, then drizzle with oil. Transfer
to a serving dish and serve immediately.

*Lagane and chickpeas
(garbanzo beans)*

For the lagane pasta:
— 400 g / 14 oz (2⅓ cups) dried
   semolina

— 250 g / 9 oz dried (1⅓ cups)
   dried chickpeas (garbanzo
   beans), soaked in water for
   12 hours
— 1 bay leaf
— 2–3 tablespoons olive oil,
   plus extra for oiling and
   drizzling
— 1 clove garlic
— 200 g / 7 oz (1¼ cups)
   tomatoes, chopped
— pinch of red chilli powder
— salt and pepper

AGNELLO ALLA LUCANA

Lucana-style lamb

Preparation time: 40 minutes
Cooking time: 1 hour
Serves 4

— 100 ml / 3½ fl oz (scant ½ cup)
  olive oil
— 300 g / 11 oz (2½ cups)
  small tomatoes, chopped
— 1–2 cloves garlic,
  finely chopped
— 200 g / 7 oz (2 cups) dry
  crustless breadcrumbs
— 100 g / 3½ oz (1 cup)
  grated pecorino cheese
— 2 tablespoons
  chopped parsley
— 1.5 kg / 3¼ lb breast or
  shoulder of lamb, cut
  into bite-sized pieces
— 600 g / 1 lb 5 oz potatoes,
  cut into wedges
— 300 g / 11 oz (1¾ cups)
  cipollina onions, chopped
— salt and pepper

Preheat the oven to 220°C / 425°F / Gas Mark 7.
Brush a baking dish with some of the oil.

Put the tomatoes, garlic, breadcrumbs, pecorino and
parsley into a bowl and mix well.

Place the lamb in the prepared dish along with the
potatoes, onions and seasoning. Sprinkle the tomato
mixture over the top and drizzle with the oil. Roast for
about 1 hour, until bubbling and browned. Serve hot.

GELATO

Legend states that Marco Polo, the fourteenth-century Venetian merchant, introduced Italy to ice cream after he brought it back from his travels in China. But whilst the origin of iced desserts can be traced back to China – where rice and milk were combined and then frozen – Italy first encountered ice cream via the Middle East. As a Persian delicacy during the summer months, ice was harvested from mountaintops and flavoured with fruit juices, rosewater and saffron. It was this sherbet drink that the Arabs introduced to Sicily in the Middle Ages, along with many other architectural and culinary influences still obvious in southern Italy today.

The appeal of *la granita* – semi-frozen dessert flavoured with lemon, coffee, pistachio or almond (as this particular region dictates) – has travelled throughout Italy; however, it was with the addition of cow's milk to the recipe that Italy's enduring love affair with gelato began. Wandering the streets of Matera in the evening, the coloured lights of the many gelaterias glow on the warm pavements. Most famous is the artisanal I Vizi degli Angeli, or the Indulgences of the Angels, a family-run shop which experiments with flavours, such as tangerine and basil; lavender; liquorice; and fig and spices.

i Vizi degli Angeli, or the Indulgences of the Angels, is an experimental and artisan gelateria.

TARALLI

Originally from Campania, *taralli* are savoury crackers made from durum wheat flour, white wine, fennel seeds, salt and plenty of extra-virgin olive oil. Like bagels, they are boiled before being baked, which gives them a unique texture, but above all means they will keep for several months. The fragrant, crunchy morsels are ideal for scooping up purées and antipasti. *Frisa* an earlier, less-refined version, rather like a doughnut made of stale bread – was probably eaten by country folk. Both are first soaked in water to soften them, the liquid is squeezed out and they are dressed with chopped tomato, oregano, salt and pepper.

On the coast, particularly around Bari, the local alternative is *puddica*, a kind of focaccia made with flour, yeast, oil, salt and oregano. The dough is pressed into a baking pan with the fingertips, then cubes of tomato and pieces of garlic are placed in the hollows and the whole thing is baked. This was especially popular with sailors and fishermen, who ate it instead of bread with their seafood. As *taralli* spread around southern Italy, they gradually became sweeter, getting as far as Andria, where they were embraced with such gusto that they are now more associated with this region than any other. The Andria version calls for white wine or Marsala, eggs and sugar, and makes the perfect afternoon pick-me-up.

Similar to the breadstick, *taralli* are a common snack in Basilicata, and are either sweet or savoury.

TAGLIOLINI DELL'ASCENSIONE

At one time, this traditional dish was customarily exchanged among neighbours to celebrate Christ's Ascension into heaven three days after his Crucifixion. In honour of the occasion, the shepherds of the Vulture area, who usually curdled their animals' milk to make cheese, instead donated it to those who made these tagliolini. Nowadays people tend to make them with cow's milk.

Ascension Day tagliolini

Preparation time: 10 minutes
Cooking time: 15 minutes
Serves 6

Pour the milk into a large saucepan, add the sugar and bring to a boil. Add the tagliolini and cook until the pasta absorbs as much milk as possible. Drain, arrange on the serving dish and sprinkle with cinnamon to taste.

— 1 litre / 1¾ pints (4½ cups) milk
— 200 g / 7 oz (1 cup) caster (superfine) sugar
— 300 g / 11 oz tagliolini
— ground cinnamon, for sprinkling

*Strawberry
sponge cake*

— butter, for greasing
— 80 g / 3 oz (¾ cup) plain
  (all-purpose) flour, sifted
— 6 eggs, separated
— 150 g / 5 oz (¾ cup) caster
  (superfine) sugar
— 80 g / 3 oz (¾ cup)
  potato flour, sifted

For the topping:
— 150 g / 5 oz (½ cup) seedless
  raspberry jam (jelly)
— 400 g / 14 oz (2¾ cups)
  strawberries, hulled
  and quartered if large
— 2 tablespoons caster
  (superfine) sugar
— zest of 1 lemon

Preparation time: 20 minutes
Cooking time: 35–40 minutes
Serves 8–10

Preheat the oven to 180°C / 350°F / Gas Mark 4. Lightly grease a deep 20-cm / 8-inch cake pan, line the base with baking (parchment) paper.

Put the egg yolks and sugar into a bowl and beat until pale and frothy. In a separate clean bowl, whisk the egg whites into firm peaks, then gently fold them into the sugar mixture in batches. Sift both the flours over the mixture and gradually fold the flours into the mixture.

Pour the batter into the prepared pan and bake for 35–40 minutes, until the sponge is golden and springy to the touch. Set aside to cool in the pan for 5 minutes, then turn out onto a wire rack to cool.

Put 3 tablespoons water into a small saucepan, add the jam (jelly) and melt over a low heat to form a syrup. Allow to cool slightly.

Put the strawberries into a bowl and sprinkle with the sugar and lemon zest. Arrange them on top of the sponge cake, then generously drizzle over the syrup.

INDEX

Page numbers in **bold** refer
to the illustrations

Phaidon Press Limited
Regent's Wharf
All Saints Street
London N1 9PA

Phaidon Press Inc.
65 Bleecker Street
New York, NY 10012

www.phaidon.com

© 2015 Phaidon Press Limited

ISBN: 978 07148 6888 2

Puglia originates from *Il cucchiaio
d'argento La Grande Cucina Regionale
Puglia e Basilicata*, first published in
2007, and from *Il cucchiaio d'argento,*
first published in 1950, eighth
edition (revised, expanded and
redesigned in 1997)

© Editorial Domus S.p.a with
the exception of recipes on pages
92 and 196 which were developed
by Anna Jones.

A CIP catalogue record for this book
is available from the British Library.

Commissioning Editor:
   Emilia Terragni
Project Editor: Michelle Lo
Production Controller: Adela Cory

Narrative text by Tara Stevens
Designed by Sonya Dyakova
Photographs by Matt Russell
Illustrations by Beppe Giacobbe
Translated by Mary Consonni

Printed in China

The publishers would like to thank
Clelia d'Onofrio, Carmen Figini,
Fred Birdsall, Anna Jones,
Susan Spaull, Theresa Bebbington,
Trish Burgess and Hilary Bird for
their contributions to the book.

RECIPE NOTES

Butter should always be unsalted.

Unless othewise states, all herbs are
fresh and parsley is flat-leaf parsley.

Pepper is always freshly ground
black pepper, unless otherwise
specified.

Eggs, vegetables and fruits are
assumed to be medium size, unless
otherwise specified. For US, use large
eggs unless otherwise specified.

Milk is always whole, unless otherwise specified.

Garlic cloves are assumed to be
large; use two if yours are small.

Ham means cooked ham, unless
otherwise specified.

Prosciutto refers exclusively to raw,
dry-cured ham, usually from Parma
or San Daniele in northern Italy.

Cooking and preparation times are
for guidance only, as individual
ovens vary. If using a fan oven, follow
the manufacturer's instructions
concerning oven temperatures.

To test whether your deep-frying oil
is hot enough, add a cube of stale
bread. If it browns in thirty seconds,
the temperature is 180–190°C/
350–375°F, about right for most
frying. Exercise caution when deep
frying: add the food carefully to
avoid splashing, wear long sleeves,
and never leave the pan unattended.

Some recipes include raw or very
lightly cooked eggs. These should
be avoided particularly by the
elderly, infants, pregnant women,
convalescents, and anyone with
an impaired immune system.